the story of **God**

understanding the BIBLE from beginning to end

the story of God

of God

understanding the BIBLE from BEGINNING to end

tommy nelson

FOREWORD BY JOSH MCDOWELL

Published in the United States of America
by Hudson Productions, Plano, Texas.

ISBN-10   1-928828-21-3
ISBN-13   978-1-928828-21-1

(First published in 1996 by Hudson Productions as The Big Picture, ISBN 1-928828-03-5)

Note: Several translations of the Bible are used in this book, including New American Standard Bible (NASB), New International Version (NIV) and King James Version (KJV). Some of these do not capitalize pronouns when referring to God. No attempt has been made to change these texts to make them uniform.

Dedication

This book is dedicated...

...to my precious wife Teresa, whose devotion, faithfulness, and encouragement have provided the nurture, support, and freedom to minister to others. Her love has been an oasis to freshen every day.

...to my sons, Benjamin and John Clark, who have done me proud!

...to a father and mother every boy should have had. To Herbert and LaVelle Nelson.

...to Ben and Janie Newman, who gave me my wife and the love and support of a second family.

Additional
tommy nelson resources

Song of Solomon
    Video Series (DVD or VHS)
    Audio Series (CD)
    112-page study guide
    The Book of Romance (book)

Song of Solomon for Students
    Video Series (DVD or VHS)
    Student study guide

A Life Well Lived (Ecclesiastes study)
    Video Series (DVD or VHS)
    Audio Series (CD)
    96-page study guide
    A Life Well Lived (book)

Additional Books by Tommy Nelson
    The 12 Essentials of Godly Success
    The Musings of an Evangelical Mind (poems) see page
    256 for sample poem

For more information call 800-729-0815 or visit
www.TommyNelsonOnline.com

Content

Acknowledgements

In the formulating of the principles and insights in these pages and in my life, I am deeply grateful. . .

...to the faithful professors of Dallas Theological Seminary who have held to the literal Word of God these many years, and who used it to root, nurture, and establish me in the truth.

...to Mel Sumrall, whose strength, guidance, example, and trust made me what I am today.

...to the saints of God at Denton Bible Church. These people are a blessed and easy yoke to bear in the Master's service. Never did a pastor tend a more delightful flock!

...to Doug Hudson, who fulfilled the vision of putting *The Story of God* on the printed page to encourage more people.

...to David McDaniel and Shatrine Krake for formatting and editing this text.

Foreword

by Josh McDowell

When I read the manuscript of *The Story of God: Understanding the Bible from Beginning to End,* I realized that God's goodness gives us hope, peace, and direction. That's a fact! When we grasp God's incredible plan for us, we are encouraged to know His love and His purpose for all of history—and for us individually.

Sadly, we live in an age of shallow thinking. In my book, *Right from Wrong,* I chronicled some of the tragic consequences of that shallowness. One of the prescriptions I recommended in that book (and which I have recommended throughout my ministry) is a return to sound, biblical truth. Unbelievers look at the thousands of pages of the Bible, and they don't understand very much at all. But many Christians don't do much better! We need something to help us step back, get a grip on the vast scope of biblical truth "from Genesis to the maps," and let the truth of the major themes of the Bible guide our lives.

That's precisely what *The Story of God* does for us. It provides a strong skeleton of the major concepts of the Bible, and then it puts meat on those bones so that we gain true wisdom, comfort, and direction. The insights in this book are wonderfully stimulating. As you read these pages, you'll probably say several times, "I never realized that before!"

Many of you will use this book for your personal study and reflection. I also encourage you to use the questions at the back of the chapters for small group Bible studies or Sunday school classes. A lot of people in your church will benefit from the challenge and encouragement of going deeper into God's Word!

The Bible changes lives. It is a lamp to show us God's way, and it is a sword which pierces deep into our hearts so we can experience God more fully than we ever imagined. *The Story of God* raises that lamp a little higher and gives you a better grip on that sword so that you will know the depth of God's love, forgiveness, and power.

For many years, my friend Tommy Nelson has been an outstanding communicator. Tens of thousands of people have benefited from his powerful ministry. Now, through the pages of this book, many thousands more will grasp the profound, life-changing truths of God's Word.

Josh McDowell
April 1996

Chapter 1

GOD'S ETERNAL PURPOSE IN HISTORY

One of the most important things I've ever learned—and which I continue to learn—is this: God has a purpose in everything that happens. He can accomplish His purpose of producing patience in me as I experience the little frustrations of life, and He can produce character in me when I face genuine calamity. But the scope of God's plan is far greater than producing fruit in an individual Christian's life. All of life and all of history make perfect sense to Him, even if they don't always make sense to you and me. He uses all things, the great and the small, to accomplish His will. In fact, behind all the seemingly pointless, confusing, and mind-boggling events of life, God is patiently working out His plan. And He is active. God's plan for man has followed a prescribed order throughout history, and it will follow His prescribed order for all eternity.

Sometimes we understand God's purposes for our lives. We sense the clear direction He wants us to go or the reason something happened to us. But in other times—many other times—we are confused about God's specific purpose in an event or a relationship. At these times, we may not understand, but we can be confident that He does. We may not be able to see the order in things, but He does. We may not have the ability to "make life work," but we can be confident that the all-wise, omnipotent, loving God knows what He's doing. And we take comfort in that. History is a record of God's goodness to man. In the pages of *The Story of God,* we will trace the goodness of God and show how our understanding of His sovereign, eternal plan brings us insight, hope, and a clear sense of direction.

Like a lot of people, I thought the Bible was a compendium of the ideas Moses, David, Job, and others had about God. But when I became a Christian and began to read the Scriptures for myself, I found it to be a narrative of history. It's not a history *man* thinks is important. In its pages, we see only one passing mention to Caesar and one prophecy about Alexander the Great. Assyria and Egypt are addressed only in relation to the people of God.

The Bible begins with the statement, "In the beginning," and ends with a book called "The Revealing," or "The Revelation." It is a fantastic look through time into eternity. The Bible describes a divine plan begun in the mind of God, and it ends with man before the face of God. It unfolds historically in time and space. Some events are purposed by God, and evil events are permitted by God. But all are a part of His divine will. In the wonderful pages of the Bible, God's plan gradually unfolds in time-space events, purposed and permitted, which ultimately result in the glory of God.

Throughout this thing we call "history," we see the demonstration of man's incontrovertible sinfulness and inarguable rebellion. We also witness the sovereign grace of God by which blinded men and women are brought near to Him. That's the message of the Bible from Genesis to

Revelation. Technically and theologically speaking, this is a study of the sovereign plan of God, but if you want to give it a more current title, you could call it, "What on earth is God doing for heaven's sake?"

Where should we begin? Should we start at the beginning of the New Testament in Matthew? The Ten Commandments and the Law? The catastrophic, worldwide flood? Should we start at the beginning of Genesis? Actually, we're going to begin our study even before that. Before the Genesis account begins, a very important set of historical events took place: the entrance of evil, the angelic creation, and the rebellion of Lucifer.

tHe pLan of God

The Shorter Version of the Westminster Confession states, "The decree of God is His eternal purpose according to the counsel of His will, whereby for His own glory, He hath foreordained whatsoever comes to pass." This statement is the best definition I've seen of "the decree of God," which is His plan to fulfill His eternal purpose in history. The outworking of history, then, is designed to demonstrate the glorious character of God.

Occasionally, somebody tells me that God created man because He was lonely. Let me assure you: God was *not* lonely. The Trinity, the perfect three in one, is never lonely. Ultimately, history is designed to demonstrate the graciousness, the goodness, the wrath, the sovereignty, the might, the holiness, the truthfulness, and the veracity of God, and to bring praise to Himself—simply because He deserves it. Man's highest good is to know this God.

Isaiah wrote, "God knows the end from the beginning." Peter said, "These were gathered together against thy holy servant, Jesus, both Herod and Pontius Pilate to do whatever Thy hand and Thy purpose predestined to occur" (Acts 4:27-28). God granted us "grace in Christ from eternity past" (II Timothy 1:9). Jesus Christ was "foreknown before the foundation of the world, but now has appeared in these last times for the sake of us" (I Peter 1:20). God's activities are sovereign. He is the sole ruler of history.

The first thing we need to know about the eternal decree of God is that it is *singular.* By singular, I mean this:There isn't a tennis match between God and Satan.There aren't two equal plans—God's and Satan's—which compete for supremacy. This give and take, however, is how biblical history appears to many of us: God created the angelic realm, but Satan fell. God created another realm, the human realm, but Satan corrupted it.Then God set up the pre-deluge world, and Satan corrupted that one too. God then destroyed the world by water. After the flood, God established government. Satan corrupted man at the tower of Babel, so God used Abraham to begin the Jewish state. Satan corrupted Abraham's descendants, and Joseph's brothers sold him into bondage through lying, deceit, and attempted murder. God later led the people out of Egypt and gave them the Law. Satan corrupted the people again and again, so God sent His final Messenger, Jesus Christ, to call the nation to repentance. But people killed Him.Through Christ's death, God established the church, but today Satan confuses people about God's Word and corrupts the church.

That sure seems like a tennis match, doesn't it? Sometimes God appears to be winning. Sometimes Satan appears to be winning. God was in control—and is in control—all the time. In the mind of God, He sees history from beginning to end. When Shakespeare wrote *Hamlet,* he knew all the scenes and acts before they sequentially appeared on stage at the Globe Theatre. In the same way, God saw all history before history as we know it ever began.

Jesus Christ came at the fullness of time, long after the origin of the universe. But God planned the Savior's advent as the pinnacle which would fulfill all that came before and give purpose to all that came after. So the decree of God is an intelligent, singular idea.Through Him, God's elect are raised from their fallen state to be presented forever as a testimony to the sovereign glory, grace, and holiness of God.

Even though the decree of God is singular, it also is *progressive*. As God's plan unfolds, two great points are demonstrated unalterably: Man is a liar and God is true. Man did not obey God's direct command in the garden, and he did not obey God when he walked by his conscience. He did not obey when God threatened him with capital punishment. Abraham, Isaac, Jacob, Joseph, and the twelve tribes had the promises of God, but they did not obey Him. Israel was entrusted with the Law, but they did not obey God. The world today has the historical fact of the resurrection and the completed Bible, but it scorns God. Christ can return and rule the earth, but ultimately those people will not obey God (Revelation 20:8-9). Finally, in Revelation 21:22, we read about God's final execution of His long awaited justice. All this progressively demonstrates what Paul said, "Let God be found true though every man be found a liar" (Romans 3:4).

God's decree is singular, it is progressive, and it also is *comprehensive*. Nothing is too large or too small for Him. God ordained the stars and calls them by name. He knows every sparrow in the mountains. He ordained His Son to go to His death, and He ordained the donkey that carried Him. He ordained the whale that swallowed Jonah, the wind that blew to create the tumult on the sea, and the little caterpillar that destroyed the gourd that grew up over the head of the grumbling prophet. God ordains evil for His own purposes, and He ordains good. At all places and in all circumstances, God can be trusted.

The Bible speaks of every area of the angelic, demonic, satanic realm, and every area of politics. It describes the earth from its dust to its stars, the sun and the moon, the metaphysical world, the moral world of good and evil, the world of God and Satan, heaven, hell, the sea, the animals, men, history, and everything from the molecules to the galaxies. We could look at Bible passages on God's sovereign control over every one of these. The plan of God is a singular, progressive, comprehensive decree.

responding to god's decree

People who understand the decree of God are thankful people. Paul wrote that we should give thanks in everything because that is God's will for us. We should be assured that "all things work together for good to those who love God." Why can Paul say these things? Because his theology was sound. God has an eternal plan, so we should completely trust Him no matter what occurs, either good or evil. Nothing occurs by accident. Events happen by the decree of God. Human events and choices please Him or displease Him, but they never perplex Him. They elicit His love or evoke His wrath; they demonstrate His grace or His judgment. All things ultimately accomplish the refining, the vindication, the examination, the purification of God's children, and they demonstrate His grace and His patience to a world that is demonstrably evil.

Those who understand the decree of God are peaceful people. Americans don't like sovereign kings, and we don't like sovereign gods, yet the Bible clearly teaches God is sovereign. If you have trouble with this, you're going to have to stay in bed with the covers up to your chin. Otherwise you will hear of evil men who break into homes and take innocent lives. Drunk drivers may cross the double lines on the highway and kill you and your family. If you don't believe God is greater than any and all of these events, even those that result in suffering and death, then you must conclude that you exist at the whim of drunkards and evil men. The sovereignty of God comforts those who believe. You and I don't need to understand all things, but we need to be assured that God is in control.

I heard a man tell of a son who was killed in a motorcycle accident. Somebody came up to my grieving friend and said, "Where was God when your son was killed?" My friend looked that person in the eye and said, "He was in the same place He was when *His* Son was killed. He was with my son, and He will use his death for His own purposes." My friend had an accurate and deep understanding that God has a plan in all things.

There's a time in every Christian's life that the decree of God becomes a glaring, demanding reality. At that moment, we have to cling to Him. The worst degrees of evil, sin, suffering, and death cannot overcome the sovereign goodness of God. Evil is culpable, responsible, and furious, but it never skirts the plans of God. That's why there are no divine apologies recorded in the Bible. God is not sin's author, but He is sin's sovereign—at its inception, in its purpose, and in its ultimate demise. God is there with me in the lions' den, just as He is there in the very presence of heaven. If we don't believe this truth, we have to become hermits because we'll believe the universe is in the hands of the wicked. But a proper view of God enables us to trust Him...just as Jesus' view of the Father enabled Him to trust as He hung on a cross.

Shoe to drop

a never ending story

The decree of God is an *eternal* plan. I Peter 1 states, "He was foreknown before the foundation of the world." Lewis Sperry Chafer was the founder of Dallas Theological Seminary. Dr. Chafer observed that Solomon built the temple over a period of 13 or 14 years, but in his mind, he saw the laying of the cornerstone as clearly as he saw the finishing of the capstone. God knows all from the beginning: all that He shall permit and that He shall cause, which essentially are the same. *Freewill*

Not only is His plan eternal, the Bible says the decree of God is *wise*. God is not a heavenly bully, nor as one atheist said, "a cosmic Nazi." God has a wise and purposeful plan which demonstrates His goodness and His grace, and He is willing to share Himself with people. This wisdom knows the role of evil to accomplish God's plan. At least one role of evil in the plan of God is to force us to wrestle with hard realities in life. When we experience evil and suffering, we recognize our desperate need for God. Without this suffering, many of us (perhaps all of us) would be shallow, self-sufficient, and petty. Our struggle with evil deepens us.

Life is like a tapestry. When a craftsman makes a tapestry, he uses greens and blues and yellows. They're pretty, but he also uses grays and blacks. These muted tones are not so pretty in themselves, but when he puts them into that whole tapestry, the total effect is quite beautiful. The same is true with the darkness of evil: it *will* have its place.

The movie *Dick Tracy* was filmed using primary colors just like the comic book: all blues and reds and yellows. The movie is a moving comic strip. It seems unrealistic because there's nothing "earthy" to it. God doesn't produce "comic strip people." In this life we have sin and suffering and death and deformity. Moses said, "God, I can't speak. I'm slow of speech." But God replied to Moses, "Who made man's mouth? Who made the blind? Did not I, the Lord?" God takes full responsibility to use our infirmities for His glory.

At Denton Bible Church, where I am the pastor, I once asked a pianist to play *Jesus Loves Me* in a major key without any sharps or flats. It was melodic, but also shallow. This version didn't demonstrate the artist's ability to play the piano. Then I asked her to cut loose and use the black keys as well. This time she added all those sharps and flats, which by themselves are dissonant. But when these notes were added, *Jesus Loves Me* took on breadth and power. Now it had grandeur, and the pianist's giftedness became clearly evident!

God's plan involves flats and sharps, grays and blacks. There are no apologies. When we don't understand, we may become angry, confused, and doubtful. David whined, "I said in my alarm, 'All men are liars!'" Jeremiah griped, "God, you've become to me a deceptive stream." But when the last chapter is written, we will understand. We will realize God deserves all praise and all glory. We say like Paul, "From you, to you, for you are all things. To God be the glory" (Romans 11:36).

The decree is *free*. In Isaiah 40:13-14, we read, "Who has known the mind of the Lord? Who became his counselor?"

Answer: nobody! The decree is built upon God Himself. It unfolds according to His purposes. It doesn't merely respond to man's rebellion.

And His plan is *unchangeable*. God doesn't alter His decree. He doesn't look at a tragic event and say, "Oops!" and then go back and change it. He doesn't make His decree contingent on anything or anyone. God's chosen people, Israel, rejected His Son and put Him on a cross, but that evil event perfectly accomplished God's ultimate plan. Lucifer rebelled and was cast out of heaven (Isaiah 14 and Ezekiel 28), and his rebellion furthered the purposes of God. Adam and Eve fell and elicited a judgment and a curse, but their rebellion took its place in the tapestry of the Bible. Because of the entrance of sin, we are introduced to God's grace. And thanks to grace, humankind is saved and brought not to a garden of Eden, but into the very presence of God.

the emotional involvement of god

God's decree also is *passable*. The word "passable" contains the idea of emotion. For His own purposes, God may permit things which displease and even anger Him. Angels and humans rebel against Him and are judged by Him, but He still emotionally responds to what He decrees. With profound regret, God judged Israel—again and again. The death of Christ was the most awful, emotion-laden event in the history of the world. Christ saw the sin and apathy of the people of Jerusalem, and He wept. Yet man's rejection of the Savior was decreed from the foundation of the world. God purposed it, but these events and these people still prompted the outpouring of God's emotions when they occurred. We should take comfort because God is displeased when evil things happen.

Years ago, my son Benjamin wanted to ride down a long ramp on his skateboard. First I got his attention: "Benjamin!" Then I issued to him my perfect will, "Do not do it!"

He said, "Aw, come on, Dad! I won't get hurt. Just this

once! Please?"

He had no doubt what my will was in this matter, yet his will was not in agreement. So I gave him my permission, within my preceptive (establishing a rule for moral conduct) and perfect (authoritative and good) will. I knew he would do what he wanted. I expected that when he did, he would learn something from his insistence on acting on his own will. I was right. He took off, against my will, but within my purposes. I was displeased, but I was also happy because my son was about to learn a valuable lesson.

I ran behind him—just waiting for the fruit of disobedence to occur! It didn't take long. *Ploomp! Bang! Blapppp!* He fell and tore himself up. While he sat there bleeding, I felt displeased, concerned, and happy. I said, "Ben, your dad's smarter than you think. I knew this would happen. Trust me. I'm not pleased, but I'm also here with you, and I'm going to care for you." I allowed him to commit evil and disobey, but through the experience, he learned about life, he learned about himself, and he learned about me. He also learned about skateboards! I had a providential watch over his actions.

Sometimes God says, "Thou shalt not!" but we're not really convinced. We do it anyway as He knew and purposed that we would. Then He runs after us because He wants us to learn something about Him, ourselves, the Bible, and sin. And the song of our lives is enriched through the black keys of experience.

God is preceptive, permissive, and providential. He can let man do whatever he wants to, but He leaves nothing to chance.

The decree of God speaks of things actual, as well as things that could be. Jesus told the people, "If Sodom and Gomorrah could have heard and seen what you have heard and seen, they would have repented in sackcloth and ashes." Saul came to kill David, and David asked, "God, will this city deliver me over into Saul's hands?" God said, "Yes." He knew what *could* occur, but it didn't because David took God's advice and left.

God's decree is _loving_. The ultimate purpose for letting Ben rebel against me was to help him learn of my love and my wisdom. Because of this lesson, he is a stronger child today. Even by allowing pain and weakness in our lives, God shows His love because He draws us to Himself. Suffering is His way of driving us from the nursery.

The decree of God is _mysterious_. Paul said, "How unsearchable are His judgments and His ways past finding out" (Romans 11:33). David said, "Such knowledge is too wonderful for me! It is too high. I cannot attain to it" (Psalm 139:6).

Once I was involved in an evangelistic outreach with a bunch of college students and singles. A philosophy student at North Texas State came the night we examined the nature of God. He asked me if I had ever studied any philosophy. I told him I wasn't fluent in the subject, but I could usually follow a discussion. He said, "Let me ask you a question." He was absolutely certain his question was the most incredible question of all time. He asked with a smile, "If God is good and knows all, then why did He create a universe that has sin, suffering, despair, and evil?"

This guy must have thought his question would discredit the Bible and cause me to turn and say, "Gosh, I never thought of that before! I think I'll become a Buddhist or something!" I just smiled and said, "Friend, how much time do you have? Do you want to look at Habakkuk, or do you want to look at Job? Would you like to look at John 11, or should we look at Romans 9 through 11? Would you like to look at Revelation 22? How about Genesis 3? How about Psalm 77 or Psalm 73? The mystery of God's will and the importance of clinging to Him in the dark is applied in the Bible to people, nations, and civilizations. It's a big issue! And the fact that God uses evil for His own purposes is the ultimate issue in the Bible."

The decree of God is _Christocentric_. Jesus is the key to God's plan. God Himself enters human history in the person of His Son. His eternal, divine Son, becomes a human just like us and suffers sin's curse. His miracles verify His claims. The gospel narratives illustrate the life of this man who fulfills the promises, the prophecies, and the purposes of God. The pinnacle of the Bible is the three years He walked with His disciples, suffered, died, and rose from the dead. In Him, evil is vanquished and Satan is crushed. Those chosen by God shall be drawn to Him and become the display case of God's glory. Jesus, the king of Israel, will return and establish all of His purposes for His chosen nation. Ultimately history will be fulfilled in the return of Jesus Christ and the establishment of His kingdom.

The decree of God is a fantastic, wonderful truth we can believe, affirm, and uphold. The famous preacher, Donald Gray Barnhouse, once preached on this subject. A man told him, "Son, I like you. You're a 'big God' preacher. I don't like 'little God' preachers; I like 'big God' preachers."

Whether we know it, believe it, affirm it, or trust it, the truth is that we have a God who sovereignly decrees all of history, from caterpillars to whales, from good to evil, from nothingness to suns, moons, and stars. He has perfect knowledge about each tiny sparrow and the expansive Milky Way. Noth-ing surprises Him; nothing confuses Him; nothing thwarts Him. That's the God we worship and love. He doesn't simply spring to action as a valet. He is not our waiter. He is not our relief pitcher when we're in trouble. He's not our fireman. He is the sovereign Lord.

The chief end of man is to know God, enjoy Him and glorify Him forever. We want to be people of the great and awesome God!

Each chapter concludes with several questions designed to encourage reflection and discussion. Some questions or exercises will help you assimilate the content of the chapter, and some will help you apply these principles to the "nitty-gritty" of your life.

Reflection/discussion questions

1. Before you began reading this book, was the thought of God's grand design for mankind stimulating, comforting, or confusing to you? Explain.

2. C.S. Lewis said "Evil is God's megaphone to a deaf world." What does this statement mean to you?

3. How do "little God" people typically respond to conflicts, tragedies, and disappointments in life?

4. How do "big God" people typically respond to these problems?

5. How would your life (your goals, relationships, motivations, etc.) be different if you were more of a "big God" person?

① ALL 3 → interest in how + why, comforting to know He is in control, confusing sin, dinosaurs + suffering.

② Their is ~~can~~ can answer (barier) - Evil
Sin can point people to Christ

③ Wonder why God would allow or wouldn't stop

④ We try to take comfort in His soverny

⑤

22. God is not Sin's Author? But did He not create everything. Did He not create Free-will. Is sin a by-product of that?

Hands of the wicked - when is it going to happen

Permit vs. cause ->

Copenhagen

Love you!
Joel!

Chapter 2

tHe anGeLIc faLL and tHe ORIGIn Of evIL

Even a casual glance through the Bible reveals the conflict between good and evil. The thoughtful reader might wonder: Where did evil originate and why does it exist? Some have concluded: If God were truly loving, He *would* get rid of evil. If He were all-powerful, He *could* get rid of it. If He were all knowing, He wouldn't have made a universe where the possibility of evil even existed.

Why would God create the world with the possibility of evil and all of its attendant horrors: starvation, plague, murder, death, wars, abortions, hatred, and genocide? Did God create an evil being to tempt us? Is evil a god in itself, as some in the East believe?

In the 4th century, Augustine stated that evil is an "ontological parasite" which necessarily co-exists with a perfect being. *Ontology* is the study of being. So what

Augustine meant is that when a Being exists who is all good, holy, and sinless, then philosophically and hypothetically there exists that which is non-good, unloving, and unkind. This evil, Augustine said, is a parasite which exists necessarily when an impeccable deity exists. But long before the creation of man, evil moved from a logical abstract to an historic reality.

messengers in high places

Where does the Bible describe the creation of a holy being whose potential rebellion could initiate evil? Was it Adam? No, evil was already on the scene when man was created. A tempter was in the Garden of Eden (Genesis 3). John tells us the identity of this serpent in his book of Revelation: "The great dragon was thrown down, the serpent of old, who is called the devil and Satan" (Revelation 12:8). This "serpent of old" is the adversary of God. Satan means "adversary." Satan was behind the serpent in the Genesis story of the temptation and fall of man.

So the question becomes: Where does Satan originate? And for the answer we must look prior to the creation described in Genesis, to the realm of the angels. "Angels" means messengers. Other titles for them include "sons of God," "sons of the mighty," "hosts of the Lord," "His servants," "burning ones," "seraphim," and "watchers."

People have always been fascinated by these creatures. Books about angels are frequently best sellers. Their work is described throughout biblical history and into the future. God names each one of them, though only Michael and Gabriel are mentioned by name in Scripture. When John saw an angel in the book of Revelation, he fell at the angel's feet. Soldiers trembled when they saw them. They're so fantastic, people are forbidden to worship them (Colossians 2:18).

The purpose of angels is to worship and serve God. They are professional adorers. Similarly, the purpose of the church is to "make known the manifold wisdom of God to the rulers and the authorities" (Ephesians 3:10). Angels watch what God does, and they glorify Him.

The Apostle Paul said he was "a spectacle...both to angels and to men" (I Corinthians 4:9). He told women in the church of Corinth to be on their most pious behavior "because of the angels" (I Corinthians 11:10). He said that salvation is something "into which angels long to look" (I Peter 1:12).

I was amazed at seminary when we studied angelology, and I wondered why we were studying something so "irrelevant." But I soon discovered that angelology is an essential part of systematic theology. In class, I received a notebook which was several inches thick. It was an incredible amount of material on the angelic realm!

Angels aid the chosen people of God. In Hebrews 1:14, the author states, "Are they not all ministering spirits sent out to render service for the sake of those who will inherit salvation?" When you get to glory, you may be met by an angel, and you may say, "Hmmm. Have I seen you somewhere before?" And he will say, "No, as a matter of fact you haven't, but I've always been there for you." He may be your guardian angel. The Psalmist said, "He will give His angels charge concerning you, to bear you up lest you strike your foot against a stone" (Psalm 91:11-12).

What is the nature of angels? They are holy, and they are as perfect as created beings can be. They are limited in knowledge and in power, yet angels always accomplish the tasks God assigns them. Angels are glorious. Whenever angels appear, people fall on their faces or tremble in fear. And angels are wise. According to I Peter, they "long to look" into the things of God.

The angelic realm is ordered. The Bible speaks of the rulers and the authorities. Michael is the "arch-," or the first, angel. Gabriel ministers to Israel. The book of Daniel describes the special angelic responsibility of looking after countries. An angel speaks of encouraging the King of Persia and bringing about God's purposes.

But angels are divided. Paul wrote Timothy, "I charge you in the presence of God, and of His elect angels" (I Timothy

5:21). These are chosen angels, but we also find many references to demons or fallen angels. Satan and his demons will never repent. The elect angels, however, will never fall. The angelic realm saw what happened at the rebellion, and they can never be deceived.

Rebellion in the Heavens

The first act of the decree of God was the creation of a race of angels who worship and serve God. But at a point in eternity past, some of those angels rebelled against God. Their rebellion incurred condemnation and they were exiled. Isaiah writes about the King of Babylon (Isaiah 14), but this king is described in terms which could only be true of someone higher than a mere human. Isaiah looked at the king who encouraged this wickedness: "How you have fallen from Heaven, oh Star of the Morning, son of dawn" (Isaiah 14:12). The phrase, "Star of the Morning," is a proper name, *Lucifer*. This name is used in Latin for the planet Venus, the brightest of all planets. Lucifer was the angel who most reflected the glory of God. He stood in God's very presence.

Verse 15 describes his evil. Notice the five-fold mentioning of the "I wills." This is the pride that brought about his condemnation. "You said in your heart, I will ascend to heaven. [He wanted a higher position.] I will raise my throne above the stars of God. [These stars symbolize the other angels. He wanted to be exalted in honor, higher than any other angel.] I will sit on the mount of the assembly. [This was the seat of the leading deity of the pagan pantheon.] I will ascend above the heights of the clouds. [He wanted his glory higher than anything in creation.] I will make myself like the Most High. [Lucifer wanted to be in the place of God. He wanted to be deity.]" This is essentially the same temptation used in the Garden of Eden: "The day that you eat of [the fruit], you shall be like God, knowing good and evil" (Genesis 3:5).

Five times we see Lucifer's sins: pride, exaltation, authority, glory, and even the desire to be God. Ezekiel 28:12, a similar text, says, "You had the seal of perfection, full of wisdom and perfect in beauty. You were in Eden, the Garden of God. Every precious stone was your covering... The workmanship of your settings was in you on the day that you were created."

Eden means "delight" and refers to God's presence. The "Garden of God" is the higher counterpart of the earthly Eden. So Satan was in both gardens. He was created holy, beautiful, and glorious, and he was unique. No other angel was like him. He was the anointed, chosen cherub. His job was not to shuttle messages to the coming human realm. His job was to be the honor guard in the very presence of God.

Notice Ezekiel 28:14: "I placed you there. You were on the holy mountain of God; you walked in the midst of the stones of fire." Lucifer could walk in the midst of the holiness of God.

Ezekiel continues: "You were blameless unto your ways from the day you were created, until unrighteousness was found in you. By the abundance of your trade, wealth, power, beauty, you were filled with violence, and you sinned. Therefore I have cast you as profane from the mountain of God. I have destroyed you, oh covering cherub, from the midst of the stones of fire because your heart was lifted up through your beauty, and you corrupted your wisdom by reason of your splendor. I cast you to the ground" (vv. 15-17). Paul accurately depicted pride as "the condemnation of the devil" (I Timothy 3:6).

We can infer that a part of the angelic realm fell with Satan in his rebellion against God. The Bible provides very little information about that event, but we see many evidences of fallen angels throughout the Bible.

the work of satan

When Lucifer and his minions fell, their natures changed and they became reprobate. God will not bring them back into His presence again. Lucifer's power is immense. The book of Jude discourages human beings from ridiculing Satan: "Even Michael the archangel did not bring a rebuke against Satan but said, 'The Lord rebuke you.'" Lucifer's work is four-fold: He opposes God; he opposes God's people; he opposes God's glory; and he opposes God's kingdom. He does it first by deception, and is called "the father of lies" (John 8:44). Every error about God and His revealed body of truth finds its origin in Satan.

When Israel went into the land and was seduced by other religions, they offered their children to idols. But behind an idol is a demon. In I Corinthians 10:20, Paul tells Christians not to eat in idols' temples. Do you know why? He says there is no such a thing as a god. Their sacrifice was actually to demons, not to gods. Paul taught that demons are behind pagan religion.

That's strong stuff! The question about other religions was very simple to David, Jesus, and the Apostle Paul. They simply would say there is one true religion. God has given us revealed truth, and everything else is deception. Satan is the father of lies in other religions.

Satan is called "the destroyer" (Revelation 9:11). He is not just the serpent; he is also the "roaring lion seeking someone to devour" (I Peter 5:8), to discredit God's people, and if he can, to kill them. Satan wants to silence their voices through death or through discrediting them. He also is called "the diablo," the accuser. In the Book of Job, Satan stands in God's presence and accuses Job. Satan says Job does not really love God. In the gospels, Jesus said to Peter, "Satan hath demanded permission to sift you like wheat, but I have prayed for you" (Luke 22:31-32). Satan's accusations are the source of many trials for you and me. Satan stands in the presence of God and accuses us day and night.

The Bible also calls Satan "the tempter" (I Thessalonians 3:5). He solicits people—particularly God's people—to commit evil and discredit their witness, which will silence their voices for good and for God.

Why in the world would God create a realm which would

have an historic fall? The answer is this: If evil did not exist, our understanding of the nature of God would be shallow. The existence of evil magnifies the attributes of God such as justice, wrath, holiness, sacrificial love, and other aspects of His nature which neither we nor the angels would have seen otherwise. *Comparison - God*

In fact, our response to suffering is the measure of our Christian testimony. Is a particular person a Christian or not? Just watch. The tempter accuses him and brings adversity. Let's see how he does in the crucible of persecution and lies. This test of suffering is how the people of God are sifted and refined. Anybody can come forward at church; anybody can answer an altar call; and anybody can be baptized; but only true children of God grow stronger through suffering, heartache, and evil. Evil is essential to the plan of God.

Actually, evil elevates God's elect from the Garden to eternity. In the Garden of Eden, Adam and Eve were alone, with a limited knowledge of God and a few appearances of God in bodily form. But in eternity, in the Eternal City, we will have a beautiful vision of God in all His glory. Where would you rather be? You can keep your garden. Give me eternity! But eternity is possible only because of Christ's redemption of sinful, evil people. Paul wrote, "Where sin increased, grace abounded" (Romans 5:20).

satan's downward spiral

Below is a summary of the seven stages of the existence of Satan. We've already covered the first two, but the final five will give you a short explanation of what's in store for him.

step 1.
Lucifer was created in glory (Isaiah 14 and Ezekiel 28).

step 2.
Lucifer rebelled and fell in sin. He became Satan (again,

Isaiah 14 and Ezekiel 28).

step 3.

Because of the corruption of Adam and Eve in the Garden, Satan is now "the god of this world," "the prince of the power of the air," and "the ruler of this world." Fallen people are called "children of wrath" and "sons of disobedience." Satan corrupted humankind so completely that when the obstetrician spanked your bottom, you were a sinner as you drew your first breath. Given time, sin bears evil fruit in our lives.

Mankind is called "those that are held captive by the devil to do his will" (II Timothy 2:26). Unredeemed man is under "the domain of darkness" (Colossians 1:13). "All the world lives in the grip of the evil one" (I John 5:19). Satan is the moving force over man's governments, and he is the agent behind pagan religion and pagan thought. Paul said that in the demonic realm there are "rulers, authorities and world forces of this darkness" (Ephesians 6:12). These are the invisible forces behind evil in the world.

step 4.

Satan was defeated by Jesus Christ. When John described the scene in Gethsemane, Jesus didn't say, "Judas is coming," or, "The Romans are coming," or, "My nation has gathered to kill me." Jesus said, "The ruler of this world is coming, but he hath nothing in me" (John 14:30). They were two champions in conflict.

Interestingly, we find only a few Old Testament references about demons, angels, and Satan. But the gospels contain many personal confrontations between the devil and Jesus. Jesus said, "The ruler of this world is cast out" (John 12:31). Paul said in Colossians, "He stripped the rulers and the authorities" (Colossians 2:15). Christ defeated them like a conquered foe, and He stripped them. Satan was defeated at the cross.

Do you remember the movie *Star Wars?* The Death Star is just like planet earth. No one can escape from it. It destroys everything. But one spot on the Death Star is vulnerable. The Alliance (the good guys) learns that a well-placed shot by a one-manned spacecraft can cause the entire Death Star to explode! The No. 1 good guy, Luke Skywalker, strikes the Death Star in that one vulnerable place, and it explodes! *Kabloom*!

Similarly, evil seems powerful and people seem helpless. We are like the Monopods in C.S. Lewis' *The Voyage of the Dawn Treader* who have one foot and can walk in one direction. Monopods slavishly adore their leader and never question anything he says. That's the plight of unredeemed man! He walks in one direction, and he completely submits to the devil. Man is weak, but he thinks he's strong. He's under captivity, but he thinks he's free. Jesus Christ is the hero who attacks the Death Star of sin—not by military might, not by education, not by science, not by medicine, and not by philosophy, but by His conquest over death in His perfect righteousness.

Satan's purpose is to enslave man, but he's losing them right and left. In Luke 11 Jesus said, "I come into the strong man's house, and I bind the strong man and take away all the armor on which he has relied, and I plunder his possessions." He defeated Satan and freed his people. And then Jesus invites us to join Him on the side that will ultimately emerge victorious.

step 5.

Someday the church will be caught up in the Rapture. The restrainer, the Holy Spirit, will be removed, and the planet will be given over completely to Satan during a time of tribulation (II Thessalonians 2). At that time, God will send to the world a deluding influence "that they might believe what is false." Satan will let all of his power reside in one man, the Antichrist, who will turn all of his hatred upon an enlightened Israel to destroy them.

step 6.

At the end of the time of tribulation, Satan is bound for a thousand years (Revelation 20:1-3). During this Millennium, man rules earth under the supreme authority of the Savior. This is as close to "heaven on earth" as you can get! "Thy Kingdom come, thy will be done, on earth as it is in heaven" is fulfilled.

step 7.

At the end of the Millennium, Satan will be released for a short period of time (Revelation 20:7-9). He will resume his work of temptation as mankind gets another chance to show obedience to God. Sadly, we are told that people will again rebel against God with Satan as their leader. At this point, God will cast the devil into the Lake of Fire with his demons and angels—and all of mankind who follow him.

That's the career of Satan: glory, fall, dominion, defeat, Tribulation, imprisonment, and then his final release and ultimate destruction.

Where does evil originate? This hypothetical premise became an historic reality in the angelic realm. Where did it find its origin? In the rebellion of Lucifer. Why does it persist? Because it serves God's purposes. The issue is not: Why doesn't God get rid of evil? Instead, the issue is: Why doesn't God get rid of evil *now*? Someday He will. I know, I've read the last chapter of the book!

Reflection/discussion questions

1. What is the average American's concept of an angel?

2. What are some characteristics of angels as the Bible describes them?

3. Does the idea of having a "guardian angel" comfort you? Why or why not?

4. What are Satan's purposes for you? In what ways is he succeeding? In what ways is he failing?

5. What do you need in order to withstand Satan's attacks so you can walk with Christ more fully?

Copenhagen

① Sitting on clouds in a TP commercial

② Towering Strength

③ Sure. While I don't think @ it often enough, When I do I see where He has protected + guided

④ destruction, to become enept
Anger, temper,

⑤ Bible, HS, time w/ God, Christian friends

Chapter 3

THE CREATION:
man in innocence

Even before the "in the beginning" in Genesis 1:1, two kingdoms already existed. God presided over the elect angels; the devil ruled the fallen ones. One angelic realm was absolutely good and righteous, and one was reprobate in its evil. They were opposite, but not equal. The kingdom of the devil was already doomed, though the final judgment wouldn't come for a while. But someday, "every knee shall bow of those who are in heaven and on earth and under the earth and every tongue shall give praise to God."

The best word I have ever read on the purpose of God and creation is by Dr. J. Dwight Pentecost of Dallas Seminary. His book, *Thy Kingdom Come,* describes the outworking of God's plan. Dr. Pentecost wrote, "The lawless rebellion of Satan against God raised a question of gigantic importance. Who is God? Who has the right to rule? The authority which had been recognized throughout God's eternal kingdom, exercised in the angelic realm had been challenged. God might have answered that question by imposing a deserved judgment on Satan and those who followed him in his rebellion (meaning immediately), and that would have conclusively demonstrated to all the subjects of God's kingdom—the angelic realm—that He alone is God, that He has the right to rule and the right to receive worship from those of His kingdom. But God sovereignly chose another method by which this question would be settled. He created the heavens and the earth."[1]

This creation was designed to provide a new sphere in which God's kingdom might be administered and through which the question of the right to rule would ultimately be concluded. The creation of man is not a re-creation. It is a creation that reestablishes and reasserts the dominion of God to the viewing angelic realm.

now for something completely different

The purpose of the creation is to make a new race which is not like the angels. They will not be a race of incredible power. These beings will be called "man," and they will be created from common dirt. Everything of their humble creation gives glory and honor to their Creator. Unlike angels who have incredible wisdom through the privilege of being in the presence of God, humankind will be given limited minds. They must relate to God by faith, not by sight. Unlike angels, people will need food to sustain them. They will have teeth to bite and tear and grind. They will have a tube with peristaltic action to move food. God will give them salivary glands to aid swallowing and digestive juices to enable them to absorb the nutrients. He will put villi into their intestines to absorb nutrients; capillaries will supply oxygen; and cells will have the ability to assimilate proteins. God created people to be dependent.

We can see only because He gave us a pair of orbs with

little openings that open and shut, with cones and rods to take in dimension and colors. The air that we breathe, the food we eat, the gravity which holds us on the earth—everything we are, have, and enjoy comes from the benevolent hand of God. Out of gratitude, these creatures ought to bow and worship Him. As a matter of fact, after God made the creation in six days, He added a seventh day for His people to give thanks and honor Him for providing food and all the other privileges they enjoy.

Creation demonstrated the wisdom, power, and benevolence of God to the angelic realm. After every day of the creation, God said, "It is good" because everything in creation was designed like a crib for this new baby known as man. Light was good. Gravity was good. The land, the air, the food, and all other created things were good—not because God needed them, not even because God was impressed by them, but because those things demonstrated His kindness to needy people.

evidence of God's wisdom

Several aspects of creation demonstrate the wisdom of God. In Genesis 1:1, we see the most primitive *foundations* of the universe. To have a universe, there must be mass. To create mass from nothing, a prime mover must be eternally existent. To have a prime mover which is eternally existent to create mass, an initial power must be active. Mass necessarily involves space. Mass and space require time. The most primitive foundations of the universe are a time-space-mass universe created by a prime mover who executes the act of creation. Genesis 1:1 states, "In the beginning [time], God [the eternal prime mover] created [exertion of energy] the heavens [space] and the earth [mass]." Time, space, mass, prime mover, initial energy—all the foundations of being are included in Genesis 1.

God then supplied the *forces* which move the creation. Our globe had no shape to begin with. It was formless and void, a watery matrix. At this point, gravitational force was created. Genesis 1:2 says, "Darkness was over the surface of the deep." When the word "deep" is used in the Old Testament, it usually refers to the ocean. But this case is an exception because the entire planet was a huge watery matrix suspended in space with the Spirit of God hovering over it. The idea of God "hovering over the face of the deep" suggests an image not unlike a mother eagle above her nest. It is a motherly term depicting God providing order and life.

Genesis 1:2 is similar to Proverbs 8:27, which says God "inscribed a circle on the face of the deep." In other words, gravity shaped the planet into a sphere. At this point, we see two primal forces: molecular and gravitational. If you know your physics, you know there is a third major force: electromagnetic, or light. In verse 3, God said, "Let there be light," and the light initially came from God Himself.

In verses 4 and 5, the watery globe is in motion on its axis, so we have one day. Incidentally, when the term "day" is used in the Old Testament, we find either the word *yom* or the word *olam*. *Olam* indicates a long period of time. But when yom is used with a numerical adjective, such as "28 days," it indicates a specific, 24-hour day. Yom is the term used here in verses 3 and 4. There was one day, a yom, which suggests to me that this indicated a 24-hour period. If so, the earth turned on its axis even before it received light from the sun, which had not yet been created.

We now examine the earth's *forms*. In verse 6 and following, we see the waters separate as a watery canopy, the "waters above," to maintain a perfect climate. Between the waters above and below was "the firmament" or atmosphere. Then the dry land separates from the waters, and land masses form. The "forms," then, include the atmosphere, land, oceans, and heavens.

But beyond all those things, God's work is seen in the *fullness* of His new creation. God created birds for the atmosphere, planets and stars in outer space, mammals on the earth, and fish in the sea. God doesn't start with one primordial animal from which all others evolved. He created a myriad of fishes, and a myriad of hamsters, a myriad of mosquitoes, and a myriad of everything else!

So we have foundation, forces, forms, and fullness, but we still lack one thing. Who's going to run God's creation? He creates a *foreman* for that task. Verse 26 and following describe how God created man. God finished the creation of the animal realm by enabling the animals to reproduce. Each species had its individual type of DNA, the genetic code. God put reproductive seed within the animals, the plants, the fish, and man. This rippling effect of life began by the hand of God, and He no longer needed to be directly involved in creation. It was finished.

We can readily see the effects of the creation, but we have to take the event itself by faith. David sang in Psalm 19, "The heavens tell of the glory of God." Paul said, "His invisible attributes have been clearly seen, understood by His workmanship" (Romans 1:20). The writer to the Hebrews stated, "By faith we believe that out of nothing God made things that are visible" (Hebrews 11:3).

Let there be people!

God supernaturally creates only one man and one woman. Man is the only creature in the animal realm in which each individual is distinctive. Each of us has unique, individualized features: shape of the face, skin tone, hair texture and color, the shape of the eyes and nose, height, weight, and a host of other subtle variations. Animals aren't so distinctive. You can't put a wanted poster up for an individual mosquito! It's even tough to find a particular German shepherd because they look very similar, but people have unique qualities which make identification quite easy.

God said, "Let us make man in our image, according to our likeness" (v. 26). The plural pronoun in this verse indicates the involvement of the Trinity. I once heard Francis Schaeffer say, "If I did not see in the Bible the teaching of the Trinity, I would be an agnostic."The triune God is one in His essential nature.That essence is identical within three individuals who are interrelated and co-eternal. All the characteristics which we deem precious in man: love, integrity, wisdom, peace, joy, patience, faithfulness, and so on, do not originate in man.They originate in God who has made man the only creature which can understand and communicate with His heart.Without the Trinity, there is no absolute reference point for the personality of man.

This truth is a large part of what it means to be created "in the image of God." God, who is loving, made a creature who is loving. God, who knows good and evil, created a creature with a conscience. In a limited sense, He gave man the freedom to choose. Man is not sovereign, but he's culpable and responsible for his behavior. God created man with a desire to know and be known. Man has a moral tuning fork of conscience which tells him right from wrong. Man is the most amazing of all of God's creations!

This created man is the viceroy on God's earth. The Puritans of the 17th century used that word, *viceroy*. Vice, vicar, vicarious, and viceroy are related terms. The vice president is vicarious, that is, in the place of the president. The Catholics speak of the Pope as the Vicar of Christ.They believe he represents Christ when he speaks *ex cathedra*. "Vice" means "in the place of." "Rey" means king, or regal. Therefore, a viceroy is in the place of the king. The Puritans taught that the glory of man is that he is in the image of God and he rules the earth as God's viceroy. All things are under his feet.The psalmist sang, "When I consider the heavens and the works of thy hands, what is man that thou art concerned with him? Yet thou has made him for a little while lower than the angels and crowned him with glory and honor and put all things in subjection under his feet" (Psalm 8). Man, created in the image of Almighty God, is a glorious creation whether he's in the womb or whether he's 90 years old on his deathbed. He can be a quadriplegic, short, fat, skinny, tall, ugly, homely, beautiful, brilliant, or retarded, yet retains a glory which is conferred on him by God Himself. He doesn't earn it; it is conferred by creation.

Verse 27 states, "And God created man in His own image, in the image of God He created him, male and female." Women have the same nobility as their male counterparts because God instills them with equal worth. In some cultures, a woman's value comes from her ability to bear children. Here in Genesis, however, her glory is secured apart from her ability to have children.

But order and authority are just as significant to the Genesis account of creation as the glory of man and woman. The Bible says the husband is the head of the family. Man is given creative authority, and the woman is his helper. He is over her like an umbrella. He cares for her, and by the order of divine creation, she submits to him. Today, many women don't like the concept of submission, but the concept is clear in the Bible. Order is divine: "Christ is the head of every man, man is the head of woman, God is the head of Christ" (I Corinthians 11:2).

God created Adam from dust and breathed life into him. Eve, however, is created from (and after) Adam so there will be no misunderstanding about who is the leader in that home. God makes her from Adam's rib so they will feel close to each other. They are equal in glory. Adam literally has his arm around her to care for her. This is a brilliant audio visual of the preciousness of woman. She sticks close to his side. For many years, pastors have quoted this accurate statement at weddings: "Not made from his head to be over him, or his foot to be under him, but his side, to be cared for by him." So man is created in the image of God. He is an individual, he is precious, he is cared for, and he is made complete with a mate in a family whose order is ordained by God.

the origin of time and work

God doesn't just institute six days of creation, establish man as the viceroy of earth and then have him crank out six days of work. God adds a seventh day for him to stop and reflect.

The Sabbath is the day which celebrates the finished work of God. The creation is finished; God is through; God is good. On that seventh day, the viceroy who rules the planet is to look upward to his benevolent Creator and love Him. The Sabbath day is pre-Israel and before the giving of the Law.

God also planted a garden in the east and named it Delight, or Eden (Genesis 2:8). Out of the ground grew every tree to supply man's physical needs. These trees "are pleasing to the sight and good for food." Incidentally, beauty, music, and craftsmanship, were all created at the same time or prior to man's creation. Art and music are divine and holy things to be used to glorify God.

In this passage, we also see the spiritual need of man. The Tree of Life was in the midst of the garden, as was the Tree of the Knowledge of Good and Evil. Why did God put the Tree of Life in Eden? Wasn't man immortal? Why did he need a Tree of Life. The fact is, only God is immortal (I Timothy 6:15-16). This means the original creation was not without death. Nature was not void of death as many people suppose. The animals had life cycles: they lived and died. Plants went to seed and died. Seasons, which implied periods of dormancy and death, were already established (Genesis 1:14).

God offered people divine life, but not through creation. It was available by faith if Adam would believe God and receive from a tree. The Tree of Life was given as a sacrament, and the Tree of the Knowledge of Good and Evil was given to test man's self-will and rebellion—the same sins which had led to Lucifer's downfall. God gave man a choice to assert his own will or trust the Word of God. This choice is embodied in God's command, "Eat of this; don't eat of that." This choice is a fork in the road in Genesis. Man is the only creature that has moral choices and is tested. The Tree of the Knowledge of Good and Evil didn't look gnarly and nasty. It was a normal, pretty tree. The Tree of Life wasn't a particularly beautiful tree with golden fruit. They looked very similar. Both looked attractive, but one leads to ruin. God wanted man to trust Him.

Adam had a choice: life or death, good or evil. Author and scholar Derek Kidner observed, "God alone has immortality. The presence of the Tree of Life in the Garden indicates that if man is to share this boon, it must be an added gift. Before the fall, between Adam and death, there stands the living God. His presence is sufficient to ward death off."[2]

All Adam had to do was go to the Tree of Life. If he ate of it and obeyed God, he would have been sealed in a holy nature just like the angelic host.

The next act in the sovereign plan of God is the temptation of Adam and Eve. What do you think happened? Surely they wouldn't turn from God! That couldn't happen, could it? God had given Adam his very existence. He gave him regency and the Sabbath day. There is no way—morally, logically, or philosophically—this man would rebel. Surely he would eat of the Tree of Life and demonstrate the honor of God to all creation. Or would he?

Reflection/discussion questions

1. God created the entire universe out of absolutely nothing. How does this fact affect your ability (or willingness) to trust God to accomplish things in your life?

2. In what ways is "the image of God" tarnished in people? In what ways is it intact?

3. What does it mean to be God's viceroy? In what ways are you actively fulfilling this role? In what ways can you serve more effectively as God's viceroy?

4. What did the Sabbath mean in the Old Testament? What does this concept mean to you today?

endnotes

[1] J. Dwight Pentecost, *Thy Kingdom Come,*
    (Wheaton, Illinois: Victor Books, 1990), p. 28.
[2] Derek Kidner, *Genesis,*
    (Downers Grove, Illinois: Tyndale Books, 1967), p. 65.

Chapter 4

THE faLL: paRaDIse LOSt

At creation God pronounced everything "good." It was a perfect, loving, benevolent creation. There was no reason the final act of creation, Adam and Eve, should not obey God. God had given them everything. In Genesis 3 we find their loyalty to God put to a test.

In some sense that we don't fully understand, Satan controlled the serpent in the Garden of Eden. Prior to the fall, the serpent had been the highest of all creatures except for man. We don't know what it looked like, but it was apparently the highest of the animal realm in intelligence (Genesis 3:1). Satan's first approach to Adam and Eve was through intellectual argument.

THIS IS a test

Notice the subtlety of Satan's deception. He came to the

woman because she was less informed about God than the man. God had created Adam and given commands to him alone. Satan alters God's Word. God had said, "From any tree of the garden you may eat freely" (Genesis 2:16). The first command from God is what Adam and Eve could do "freely." Yet Satan pointed not to all that they *could* do, but rather to the one thing that was forbidden. He looked only at God's restriction, not His freedoms.

Notice something else in Genesis 2:4: the name "God" is always prefaced by the term "Yahweh," translated in most Bibles as "Lord." This is the divine, personal name God assumes in the creation account of man. That name, Yahweh, is Hebrew for, "I will be what I will be." It's the perfect name for God, and the one God used later to answer Moses' question, "What is your name?" God is a holy being who can only be known by what He says and does. We cannot "know" God using only logic or philosophy. He is the living God who discloses Himself, therefore His name, Yahweh, is used throughout Scripture to signify His personal relationship with man.

Yet when Satan tempted Eve, he didn't use the name "Yahweh." In Genesis 3:1-7, the name "Elohim" is used. "Yahweh" is not used again until after the fall (when the Lord God was walking in the garden) because it is much harder to sin against a God who loves, creates, and tells you who He is. In this way, the serpent made God impersonal—not the One who revealed Himself in creation.

When the woman responded to the serpent's initial temptation, she misquoted God's previous instructions. First she said, "From the fruit of the trees of the garden we may eat." She dropped a word because God had said, "You may eat freely." She also said, "From the fruit of the tree in the middle of the garden, God has said, 'You shall not eat it or touch it.'"

God had made it clear that eating its fruit would lead to death, but He had never said, "You shall not *touch* it." This was the first act of religious legalism: adding rules that God had not imposed. God gave His people lots of freedom! In essence, He said, "You can touch the tree, climb the tree, carve your initials in the tree, and hang a swing from the tree. Just don't eat of it!'"

Eve was also a bit more casual about the consequences of disobedience. She told the serpent that God had said not to eat the fruit, "Lest you die." What God had really said was, "On the day that you eat it you shall *surely* die" (2:17). The Hebrew translation for this is, "die die." Or we might translate it as: "You shall be absolutely, most assuredly, irrevocably, inexplicably dead! You will be physically dead and spiritually dead, separated from Me if you decide to do it." Eve, however, wasn't as stern about the nature of justice.

Satan had already questioned the integrity of the Word of God. Now, in Genesis 3:4, he denies the justice of God by boldly asserting that God's Word is not true. "The serpent said to the woman, 'you surely shall not die.'" All he did was transpose two little words and add one, but this changed the entire meaning. God said, "You surely shall die." Satan said, "You shall surely not die." He was just as emphatic about the fact that God was wrong about the consequences of sin as God was emphatic about the assuredness of death. Satan tried to delude Eve into believing sin was not so bad, and that there would not be ultimate judgment for evil.

Satan then blasphemed the character of God by implying that God was not good and that Eve would miss out on the fullness of life if she listened to Him (vv. 4-5). In verse 5, Satan boldly attacked God: "God knows that in the day you eat from it, your eyes will be opened and you will be like God, knowing good and evil." Satan questioned God's Word, God's justice, and God's nature. He started the temptation with an affirmation, rearranged a few words, and ended up blatantly opposing God. He's skillful at lying and deceit! He convinced Eve that evil was really good and that what God said was actually bad, and also, that she would never really live until she renounced God's authority.

Satan continues to deceive people today. Many people are attracted by God's offer of forgiveness and a changed life, but Satan slyly convinces them to put off a decision and "live a little" first. The thought is: "You will deny the ultimate purposes in life if you are obedient to God. To really experience life, you need to do your own thing and obey your own passions." When I encounter people with this opinion, I tell them they have made three wrong assumptions:

1. obedience to God is bad.
2. disobedience will be fun.
3. they will be alive tomorrow to make the decision to trust Christ when it's more convenient for them.

These are assumptions that Satan must sell in order to succeed. Eve saw an evil thing as good. She rejected God's truth and followed her deluded reasoning. She rejected God's Word and followed Satan's seemingly logical—but eternally destructive—way of thinking. That's the mastery of Satan's temptation. Eve was not *forced* to do anything at all. She *willingly* acted and convinced herself that what she was doing was good.

She ate and then gave the forbidden fruit to Adam. The Bible never says that Adam was deceived. Eve was deceived, but Adam sinned knowingly and willfully (Romans 5:12). Some people suggest that Adam wanted to follow his wife no matter what happened to her. One of my friends says he thinks Adam watched Eve to see if she would fall over dead after eating the fruit. When judgment was not immediate, he decided to eat it, too. The desire for immediate gratification sounds familiar, doesn't it?

What would have happened if Adam had not eaten the fruit? Perhaps Eve would have died, and God would have created another woman. We don't know. The fact is that Adam "listened to the voice of his wife" instead of loving God over his own life and even the thing most precious to him.

tHe test Results: a faiLinG GRade!

The first act of religion is described in Genesis 3:7. After

Adam and Eve sinned, they realized they were naked before God. They felt guilty, and they tried to hide their own nakedness with their own good deeds. With their own efforts, they made fig leaves into a covering.

Then, immediately, came the first picture of salvation (v. 8). Man didn't seek God—because God wasn't lost! God sought out man. Adam and Eve feared Him because they knew they were guilty, so God called to them and demanded honesty: "Who told you that you were naked? Did you disobey?" Notice the beauty of salvation in this passage! Man covered his own guilt, but God sought him anyway.

But Adam didn't want to admit his own guilt. He blamed Eve! "The woman whom thou gavest me, she gave me from the tree and I ate" (v. 12). Beneath this statement is the suggestion that, "I'm not responsible. And really, God, it wasn't even my wife's fault. *You* gave her to me. I didn't ask for her. It's *Your* fault!" That's the way people are. When we are guilty, we try to save ourselves by pointing the finger at someone else.

Note that in the fallenness of this first family, the woman assumes spiritual leadership (v. 13). Eve was more honest than Adam. She said to God, "The serpent deceived me. I am guilty." And after her admission of guilt comes the passage known as "the curse." The Apostle Paul said in Romans 8:20, "The creation was subjected to vanity, not of its own will but because of Him who subjected it in hope." This important verse tells us that creation was not corrupted at the beginning. There was an activity of God to curse it, but He cursed it with the "hope" of someday setting it free. The death, decay, and violence we see around us is not the creation God originally made, and it's not the creation that will be. But for now, we live under the curse, because judgment was not limited to Adam and his family. The entire creation experienced a fall because of the sin of its head, Adam.

First, God cursed the serpent, the instrument of sin: "Because you have done this, cursed are you more than all cattle, more than every beast of the field. On your belly you

shall go, and dust you shall eat all the days of your life"
(v. 14). In Isaiah's description of Christ's Kingdom, the lion
lies down with the lamb, and the curse is lifted. Isaiah says,
"And the serpent shall eat dirt" (Isaiah 65:25).The serpent is
the one animal from which the curse is not lifted in the reign
of Christ.

God also cursed the woman:"I will greatly multiply your
pain in childbirth" (v. 16). Every time that a woman gives
birth, she is reminded that something is instinctively wrong
with this child. He or she is fallen. From the very opening of
its mouth, the child utters a cry. In Psalm 51:5, David states,"I
was conceived in sin, and I was brought forth in iniquity."

God also said,"Your desire shall be for your husband, and
he shall rule over you."The word for"desire"is used two other
times in the Old Testament. It's a strong word in the Hebrew,
and it speaks of something totally consuming something else.
The word is used in the Song of Solomon about the sexual
passion that a man and a woman have for each other."I am my
beloved's and his desire is for me" (Song of Solomon 7:10). Is
that what the curse is: that in spite of the woman's bringing
forth children with pain, she would have an incredible sexual
passion for her husband? No, this is not the "desire" in this
passage because the context doesn't fit.

The same word is used one chapter later the first time
sin is mentioned (Genesis 4:7). God told Cain, "If you do not
do well, sin is crouching at your door, and its desire is for
you, but you must rule it." Sinful desire is like an animal that
threatens to destroy you. From this point, the woman will not
be naturally submissive to her husband. Her desire will be to
dominate her husband, but he is the head by divine dictate.

Submission is not understood simply by the order
of creation. Instead, it is also imposed as a dictate from God.
I asked my wife: "Teresa, does this passage mean what it
appears to mean? Because of the fall of man and of woman,
do you have an innate desire to rebel not only against God,
but against *moi*? Do you want to take the reins of this family
from me, the one who loves you?"

Teresa responded with a smile, "Why do you think the Bible commands me in Colossians, Ephesians, and Titus to submit to you?"

Most of us resist authority, so God has to mandate how we should act. Kids don't like to submit to parents, so God commands them to submit to their parents just as He commands us to submit to the government and to our bosses. And God commands the woman to submit to the man, even though that is not her inclination or desire.

People are frequently critical of the Apostle Paul's views on submission. But submission started as God's idea in Genesis. God decreed submission by creation's order and mandate.

In verse 17, the ground is cursed. It will bring forth thorns and thistles. On the cross, the last Adam, Jesus Christ bore on his brow a crown of thorns when He was cursed.

And in verse 19, not only is the ground cursed, but so is the man. In effect, God tells him, "Eden is not yours anymore, Adam. You are out of the garden. You will have to sweat out a living." The consequences of sin were extensive indeed.

However, God explained that a perfect kingdom will someday be reestablished. If I asked you where in the Bible Jesus Christ was first mentioned, would you have an answer ready? You should. It's right here in Genesis 3:15 where God addresses Satan: "I will put enmity between you and the woman, between your seed and her seed. He shall bruise you on the head, and you shall bruise him on the heel."

Three things are included in this text. First, there will be two groups of people on the earth: the seed of the serpent (the children of the devil) and the seed of the woman (the children of God). Second, those two groups have natural enmity and hatred for each other. Third, a singular man, "He," will crush the head of Satan so hard that he'll wound himself in the process. He will not merely inflict pain on Satan; he will destroy him.

We need to ask a couple of questions. Who is "the seed of Satan?" Paul calls mankind "sons of wrath, children of disobedience" (Ephesians 2:1-3). By our very DNA, we are disobedient to God, and we are destined for wrath and judgment in hell. Our destiny is one of hopeless condemnation. Man will not and cannot come to God on his own. All aspects of human nature are cursed: his intellect, will, and body are darkened, perverted, and doomed. This is what theologians call "total depravity." So the "seed of Satan" are mortal men. Some will sin less, some will sin more, but they all rebel. They are all in need. They don't need religion; they need forgiveness and rebirth. What does it take to get into the kingdom of God? You must be. . . improved? No, "born again." You must abandon this family and be born into another family, the family of God.

And who is the "seed of the woman" who will conquer Satan? It is a man, and oddly enough, the man's lineage is traced from a woman. When men are mentioned, their genealogy is traced through the male. This person, however, will be "the seed of woman" because He doesn't have a human father. He is virgin born. He is going to come from heaven through the vehicle of Mary, and He is going to defeat Satan at the cross. In Revelation 20:10, He will cast Satan into the Lake of Fire.

In other words, from the very moment of sin, God declared how He would remove sin. It's not going to be through reincarnation! You're not going to be born back into humanity by building up "good karma" in your past life. You're not going to get to heaven because you do more good works than bad works. No! One male will stomp Satan so hard He will crush his head. From these sons of the devil, God will take a remnant, touch their hearts, and "transfer them from the domain of darkness into the kingdom of God's dear Son" (Colossians 1:13).

Not long ago, I spoke at the University of North Texas at an open forum in one of the dorms, and a young man raised his hand. He said, "How can you claim Christianity is the only way to God when there are so many other religions and they all predate Christianity?"

I said, "Excuse me. The oldest of all religions is the one which was initiated one sentence after the edict of cursing. In that statement, God defines the way Satan will be defeated. Victory will be gained by one holy man who will crush the serpent's head. The oldest of religions is Christianity. And when you consider that the solution to man's fallenness started before time began in the mind of God, Christianity is infinitely older than all religions. I am saying that Christianity, Jesus Christ, is the only way to God. If He isn't, there better be somebody else out there who was virgin born, died, rose from the dead, and ascended to heaven. From the very outset of our Bible, God dictated that victory will come through the Christ."

Immediately after the first prophecy of Christ is a picture of salvation. Adam deserves death, but he is allowed to live because an animal dies in his place. This is the first example in the Bible of "substitutionary atonement."

How is man going to respond? Do you think he will submit to this promise? We'll see in the next chapters.

Reflection/discussion questions

1. Describe the sequence of Satan's temptation of Eve.

2. Why do you think Adam sinned knowingly?

3. How did Adam and Eve respond when God confronted them with their sin? What are some ways people typically respond to the reality of their sins?

4. List areas of your life which have been specifically affected by the curse.

5. What are some specific temptations Satan uses on you? How do you normally respond to each one? What do you need in order to effectively resist temptation?

Chapter 5

man undeR conscience: tHe pRe-flood woRld

Three ideas surface in Genesis 3 which are found throughout the Scriptures, both the Old and New Testaments. They form the foundation of God's plan of salvation history. They are:

1. A promise about a Messiah.
2. Two groups of people (the children of God and the children of the devil).
3. A picture of substitutionary atonement through the shedding of blood (when God replaces fig leaves with animal skins).

tHe BIRtH of institutions

In Genesis 4, these concepts become institutions. In

verses 1 and 2, we see that the promise of the Redeemer is continued. Eve has a child she thinks is the Redeemer, the child promised in Genesis 3:15. "Now the man had relations with his wife Eve and she conceived and gave birth to Cain." "Cain" is the Hebrew word for "begotten." She said, "I have begotten a man-child with the help of God." She thinks God gave her the child-redeemer, but she realizes by verse 2 that any child conceived of man is conceived in sin and brought forth in iniquity. Children can really help clarify your theology about sin!

In verse 2, Eve names her next child "Abel," which means "vanity." Abel is the keeper of the flocks (which signifies man's position before sin). Cain is a tiller of the field (which signifies man's position after sin). This is symbolic. One is a child of God; the other is a child of the devil.

The institution of sacrifice begins in verse 3: "It came about in the course of time that Cain brought an offering to the Lord of the fruit of the ground, and Abel on his part brought forth the firstlings of his flock, the shedding of blood and their fat portions." Two peoples emerge. In the New Testament, John wrote, "By this the children of God and the children of the devil are obvious. The one that does evil is not of God, nor the one that hates his brother. For this reason Cain slew Abel." Why? What was the reason? "Because his deeds were evil and his brother's were righteous" (I John 3:10, 12). John looked at Cain and Abel as the emblematic sources of the two races which proceeded from the Garden of Eden.

Abel offers up the gift by faith. In Hebrews 11:4, God looks at his heart and he sees a heart of love and repentance. About Cain, it says in verse 4, "God had no regard" for Cain and his offering. God literally "did not look" upon Cain's sacrifice. The main reason is, as the book of Proverbs states, "The sacrifice of the wicked is an abomination to God." Wicked men who carry on their religious acts are abominable to God. God isn't impressed that someone merely shows up at church. He sees the person's heart. This person may give money to God, but in his heart he resists God, he defies Him, and he lies to Him.

God sees his unrepentant heart, and He isn't impressed by empty religious acts.

In every congregation, there are Cainites. They are in contempt of the Word of God, contempt of the justice of God, and contempt of the people of God. They just go through the motions. And like Cain of old, God is not impressed with modern Cainites. He sees right through it.

God rejected Cain's sacrifice, and Cain's countenance fell. He was unhappy, but he refused to repent. So the Lord said to Cain, "Why are you angry? Why has your countenance fallen? If you do well, will not your countenance be lifted up?" If you don't do well (repent), sin will destroy you. This is the first mention of the word "sin" in the Old Testament, and it is pictured as an animal which can devour a person. You can not peacefully cohabit with it. You have to master sin or it will consume you.

God simply commanded the people of that day to do good. There was no written law; they lived by conscience. They were to honor their innate moral barometer which told them when they sinned. If they sinned, they were to repent and trust in the sacrifice. From the time of Adam, God instituted sacrifices as the means to approach Him. And that's what Cain should have done.

tHe woRLd's fiRst muRdeR mysteRy

But we all know the story. Cain murders his brother Abel. God confronts him (v. 9). At least Adam admitted his evil (though he tried to blame his wife). Look what this man does: "And the Lord said to Cain, 'Where is Abel your brother?' And he said, 'I do not know.'" Cain lied to God, and then in scoffing he asks, "Am I my brother's keeper?" Abel was a keeper of the flocks, and Cain had contempt for shepherds. He asked God, "Do I have to look after him like he looked after those stupid sheep? No way!" And God says, "I saw what you did and the ground cries out for blood, and so it's going to punish you, and it will not yield its produce. You are banished from the presence of the Lord."

Incidentally, the birth of Seth (who replaced Abel) occurred 130 years after the creation of Adam (Genesis 5:3). So in those 130 years, there were other children of Adam and Eve, and obviously, they intermarry. God instructed Adam to "be fruitful and multiply" and he did. In 130 years, the region became populated. Apparently, marrying within a family was permitted by God at that time. The practice, however, was later banned for obvious reasons.

God banishes Cain from His presence as a lesson to all men, and Cain is told to wander. "Nod" is the land of "wandering" east of Eden. "And Cain had relations with his wife and conceived and gave birth to Enoch." Enoch is the Hebrew word "dedicated." Cain then "builds a city and calls the name of the city Enoch, after the name of his son." That is an act of defiance! Cain effectively declares, "I *will not* wander, I *will* have a city, and I *will* name it after my son." This is the formation of the first recorded city.

Where do you go to get away from evil? Do you say, "Hey, let's move to Dallas or Denver or New York?" No. In the pursuit of peace and quiet, people go to some small hamlet to get away from the mob of the city. The first city described in the Bible became wicked. The next city is Babel in Genesis 11, and it's wicked too. Lot gets seduced by Sodom, the wicked city. Jesus wept over the city of Jerusalem which rejected Him. It's with good reason that John the Baptist cries out in the wilderness for people to come out of the city to him. It's for good reason that Jesus Christ arose in the morning and went out to a lonely place to pray. There's only one city and one civilization in the Bible which is holy, and that is the city "whose architect and builder is God." That's all. Just one. Beware "the city" of man.

tHe BeGInnInG of cIVILIzatIon

There were seven generations from Adam to Noah, but see what civilization becomes. We're looking here at the first civilization, but you'll find it's suspiciously familiar to the life described in your local morning news! This is what happens when lots of sinful people get together: They don't obey their consciences, and they don't seek the substitutionary provision of God. They pursue their own desires.

For example, Lamech took to himself two wives (Genesis 4:19). Hello! Two wives? What did Genesis 2:24 say? "For this cause a man shall leave his father and mother and shall cleave to his wife." Wife. Singular. Lamech rejected the command of God about the family. Adah gave birth to Jabal, a rancher, and Jubal, an artist. Zillah's child was Tubal-Cain, the founding father of technology and industry. These, then, were the foundation stones of civilization: raising cattle, the arts, and industry.

Civilization advanced in the ability to subdue the earth, but people subdued it without God. This was the first humanistic society. Technology advanced, but at the same time, sin increased. "Lamech said to his wives, Adah and Zillah, listen to my voice, you wives of Lamech, give heed to my speech. I have killed a man for wounding me, and I have killed a boy for striking me." Lamech was a murderer as well as an adulterer. Behold the contempt of God! Was Lamech in awe of the edict of the God of justice? Was he afraid of hell and judgment? No chance! Lamech says he's tougher than God: "If Cain is avenged seven-fold, then Lamech seventy-seven." "Bring it on!" he says. "I can take it!"

In the first civilization, technology and the arts advanced, but morality, the home, and revealed truth were pushed aside. Every civilization that has ever existed—Egypt, Assyria, ancient Babylon, current Babylon, Persia, Greece, Rome, Dallas, America—follows the same trend. In his innate brilliance, man can perfect the arts, poetry, media, technology, industry, and ranching. He can subdue the planet. But things of true value are held in contempt.

Look at America today. Technology is much more developed than it was in Ruth's day, but we haven't improved on Ruth's character. The modern fishing industry can do better than Peter's net, but we haven't improved on Peter's heart. Technology has advanced in unprecedented ways, but our country has gone downhill morally and spiritually—just as in Genesis 4 and 5!

Was the rule of God established when conscience called man to repentance and sacrifice? The answer is no. Man becomes humanistic, murderous, immoral, and defiant of God. Innate morality simply won't work.

At this point in the game, Satan seems to be winning. But we're not finished. Eve gave birth to another son and named him Seth, which means "appointed," for she said, "God has appointed for me another offspring in the place of Abel" (Genesis 4:25). Seth is special. He takes the place of Abel. As the gospel of Luke traces the genealogy of Jesus Christ, it goes back to Seth, and the righteous line continues.

To Seth was born a son, Enosh (the Hebrew word for "frailty"). Seth realized he lived in a wicked generation. He felt weak; He needed God. Verse 26 says, "Then men began to proclaim the name of the Lord." In opposition to the wicked generation, a group of men proclaimed Yahweh. They were children of God, light and salt to their world.

Genesis 5:21-24 introduces us to another man named Enoch, who is mentioned twice in the New Testament, once in Jude and once in Hebrews 11. He's an important fellow. Why? He's the first prophet and has a revelation from God about coming justice. This righteous lineage in Genesis 5 is typical of God's people. They herald the name of God with boldness because they have a revelation from God of coming justice and a coming Redeemer.

Verse 21 says, "Enoch lived 65 years and became the father of Methuselah, and Enoch walked with God 300 years after he became the father of Methuselah." There's something about the birth of Methuselah which brings Enoch close to God. Enoch has a revelation from God that judgment on this wicked world of Lamech is coming. Enoch knows that people need to get ready. Jude 14 states, "About the wicked, in the seventh generation from Adam, Enoch prophesied saying,

'Behold the Lord came with many thousands of his holy ones bringing judgment upon all and convicting the ungodly of their ungodly deeds, done in an ungodly way.'"

How did Enoch become a prophet? At the birth of Methuselah (Methuselah means "when he dies, judgment"), God let Enoch know judgment was coming. And three generations later, a son is named Noah, or "rest," because he will give people rest from the curse. They think he is the redeemer, but he's not the final redeemer from the final judgment. He is a temporal redeemer from a temporal judgment: the flood. Noah is a "type" of the final Redeemer.

So what kind of people are these? They are weak, but they are bold in their spirits. They have a revelation from God, and they know judgment is coming. They live in hope and holiness. Enoch "walked with God." This righteous man exemplified a holy people who were light and salt in their day. The Bible makes an amazing statement about this man: "Enoch walked with God; and he was not, for God took him" (Hebrews 11:5). He was raptured! Gone! In his day, he provided hope that people who believe in God will not see death. What a way to go!

The Bible tells us about three raptures: Enoch before the flood; Elijah before the judgment of the Northern Kingdom; and believers at Christ's return prior to the final judgment.

So far, we've seen rebellion from individuals (Adam and Eve), and from the civilization which came from them. In the next three chapters, God wipes everyone out and starts all over with Noah and his sons. A new restraint is implemented. Instead of letting man live by conscience, God states, "Whoever sheds man's blood, by man shall his blood be shed." Capital punishment will be instituted, and government will have the responsibility to take life and to enforce the rule of God through fear. So what effects do you think these changes will have on people and cities? Read on and find out.

reflection/discussion questions

1. How did God provide for Adam and Eve's sin?

2. If you had been Adam or Eve, how would you have felt about:

   ...the blood sacrifices for your sin?
   ...the promise of a Redeemer?
   ...each other?

3. Why do you think Cain killed his brother?

4. In light of technology's empty promise to improve people, how should Christians respond to our culture's technological and information revolution?

5. In what ways is conscience a reliable guide for us? In what ways is it unreliable?

Chapter 6

man under
government

If you were to ask a group of Bible teachers what are the most enigmatic passages in the Bible, they might point to one of three texts: Hebrews 6, Romans 9, and Genesis 6:1-4. The Genesis 6 passage contains several difficult phrases. Let's take a look at it.

"It came about when man began to multiply upon the face of the land and daughters were born to them, that the sons of God saw that the daughters of men were beautiful, and they took wives for themselves, whomever they chose. And the Lord said, 'My Spirit shall not strive with man forever, because he also is flesh. Nevertheless, his days shall be 120 years.' Then Nephilim were on the earth in those days, and also afterward when the sons of God came into the daughters of men and they bore children to them, those were the mighty men who are of old, men of renown."

Who are the sons of God? Who are the daughters of men? Who are the Nephilim who were on the earth in those days? What does God mean when He says, "My Spirit will not strive with man forever"? These are difficult questions.

One time when I taught the book of Genesis and got to this passage, I placed two chairs by the pulpit. I brought all the volumes I found which describe the two predominant views on this text. I stacked one chair full of books that held one view, and I stacked the other chair full of the alternative view. Both views are defended by good, godly scholars of the Bible. The two views are not separated along the lines of liberals and fundamentalists. Even at Dallas Theological Seminary where I received my training, different professors hold different views.

perusinG confusinG views

One view says this passage refers to the intermarriage of the lines of the righteous and the wicked. Nephilim means "men who fall" or "fallen ones." To "fall" can imply murder, such as "falling on" another person. Nephilim, then, were violent men.At that point, the voice of God was stilled and the light of the world from Seth to Noah was darkened because of this intermarriage.This set the stage for the flood.

The problem with this view is that it isn't consistent with the normal meaning of "sons of God" throughout the Old Testament. The term "sons of God" usually refers to the angelic realm. Job 1:6 says "the sons of God came to present themselves before the Lord." Again in Job 38:7, "The sons of God shouted for joy" at the laying of the foundations of the earth.The Psalmist said, "Sing to the Lord, sons of the mighty. Sing to the Lord, glory and strength." Generally, "sons of God" refers to angels—especially when it is used prior to the time of Abraham and Israel.

The historic Jewish view is that "sons of God" are fallen angels who followed Lucifer in his rebellion—demons who assumed human form. During this earthly period, these fallen angels came to the daughters of men and made an offer to them of immortality. This event can never be repeated. Fallen angels are forbidden to assume human form. It's a boundary that God has put on the demonic realm because mankind cannot tell the difference between a demon and an angel. But God said, "My Spirit will not abide (or strive) with man forever." (The term "strive" can be interpreted "abide," as Kidner does in *The Tyndale Commentary*.) If this concept is accurate, it fits nicely, though perhaps still enigmatically.[1] Intermar-riage with angelic beings won't produce immortality because man is only flesh, so God set a time of 120 years, after which the earth would be destroyed by the flood.

I believe this construction best fits the text, as well as in the New Testament. This is the one occasion in the Old Testament where angels "left their own domain and abandoned their personal abode" (Jude 6 and 7), and God judged them. These fallen angels offered man immortality, and the subsequent union led to God's decision to send the flood to a wicked earth.

I do not understand the metaphysics of how an angel co-habits with a human, but faith is not built upon questions the Bible does not answer. Rather, faith is built upon what the Scripture clearly tells us.

The book of Jude is written about erroneous and heretical teachers who deny the promise of God's judgment. Jude refers first to the example of Israel coming out of Egypt when God destroyed the entire generation of unbelievers. His conclusion was that God *does judge* because He *did judge* an entire generation. Secondly, God judged disobedient angels because they violated His boundaries. They "abandoned their proper abode," and therefore, He has kept them "in eternal bonds under darkness for the judgment of the great day." They have now been removed from their ability to tempt ever again, and they have been placed, as the text says, "in eternal darkness." Verse 7 provides a third illustration: "Just as Sodom and Gomorrah and the cities around them, since they in the same way as these."What does "these" refer to? It refers to the antecedent noun: the angels. Jude compares the sin of Sodom and Gomorrah to the sin of those angels.

How did Sodom and Gomorrah compare to the sin of the angelic realm who left their own abode and their own domain? Both involved two peoples not meant to cohabit: men with men in Sodom and Gomorrah, and people with angels in Genesis 6. Both pairings were strange and grossly immoral.

It's easier to hold to the first interpretation, a Seth-Cain intermarriage, because it's not quite so fantastic. This second interpretation of Genesis 6:1-4 *is* fantastic! I believe the Bible teaches that as death began to occur on the earth, the satanic realm made an offer. Fallen angels assumed humanity and took wives. They produced Rosemary's babies. Yes! That's exactly what it teaches. It seems incredible, I know, but look at what the New Testament has to say about it: "God did not spare angels when they sinned" (II Peter 2:4). What was the sin of angels? We're back to the book of Jude: "They abandoned their own domain and did not keep their own abode" (vv. 6-7). I believe when "The sons of God came unto the daughters of men," that's when fallen angels crossed the line and sinned.

This sin of "the sons of God" and the daughters of men produced an evil that was unlike anything the world had ever seen or will ever see again. One hundred years later, God had to destroy the face of the whole earth except for Noah and those on the Ark.

LOOKS LIKE ITS GOING TO RAIN!

So, why is this text in the Bible? These four verses describe the evil of the world which precipitated the flood. This Satanic intervention in offering man immortality without God brought on the flood of Noah.

The flood is important for three reasons. First, the flood teaches that God will judge evil even when we may think He is blind to it. Second, we see that God saves the faithful in the midst of evil. Noah is one of the great pictures of Jesus Christ in the Bible. The flood and judgment come quickly unexpectedly, and there is salvation found only by putting faith in a man who is counted righteous. By faith in him, believers are lifted up above the floods of judgment. It also looks utterly foolish! Noah builds a craft of wood in a landlocked country. But faith in the foolishness of God allows people to escape the judgment which sweeps the earth. And third, this passage teaches that God won't judge the earth like this any more. He made a promise, and He gave us the rainbow as a reminder of that promise. Man need not fear a worldwide cataclysm anymore. He now only needs to ponder the return of Jesus Christ!

Meteorologists tell us that we can't have a 40-day flood on earth today. It's impossible. We have enough moisture in our atmosphere to produce only about one centimeter of water all over the world. Noah's culture had a flood for 40 days because the atmosphere was different than it is now. Genesis 1:4 and following explains that there were waters above the earth which were separated by the atmosphere from the waters beneath. The earth was a perfect environment; a vapor canopy surrounded the earth. All of a sudden "the chambers of the deep" opened, and the result was 40 days of flooding. When Noah walked down the gangplank of the Ark after the flood, the world was not the same as it was when he got in the boat. The absence of the vapor canopy blanket caused dramatic changes in climactic conditions, and eventually, polar regions, deserts, temperate areas, and tropical rain forests developed.

Genesis 9 contains the "Noahic Covenant," the promise of God never to destroy the world through flood again. At this point in the biblical narrative, we have seen three covenants of God. In the Garden of Eden we saw the "Edenic Covenant" in which God promised man could rule over the earth. The fall shattered man's position, but one day this rule will be restored in Jesus Christ, whom God raised from the dead and gave authority over all things. The second covenant was the "Adamic Covenant" in which God promised that One will come from the seed of woman to crush the serpent's head. This covenant is the promise of redemption in Christ. In the "Noahic Covenant," God promised restraint. He will never destroy the creatures of the earth by water again.

I believe God gave this promise because He knew how paranoid we would become. If we saw a volcano erupt, we would say, "Oh no! This is it!" If we saw the sky cloud up and rain, we might think, "It's happening again!" If we saw lightning, we might yell, "God is destroying us again!" People would always be running around, neurotic, ready for the end of the world! But God promised in Genesis 8:21, "I will never again curse the ground on account of man," and here's why, "because the intent of man's heart is evil from his youth."

In essence, God is saying, "Man will never, ever improve, and he will always be afraid that I will strike the earth in judgment again." So God raises His right hand and He says, "I swear to you, I'll never, ever surprise you in judgment. I'll telegraph you and tell you how I'm going to do it in Revelation, but I'll never surprise you by a natural catastrophe again."

What's the sign that God gives the earth that He will never destroy the earth again? God says, "I'll set my bow in the clouds." A rainbow occurs when it quits raining and the sun shines through. Water vapor in the sky makes a prism, and that prism separates the colors of the spectrum in a brilliant display of a rainbow. God says, "This is my sign that the rain is over." When He says, "I'll set my bow in the clouds," God uses the same word in the Old Testament for an archer and his bow and arrow. God means He will lay aside His instrument of judgment. He will put it in the clouds, and He won't use it. Every time the rains stop and the sun shines, we see this bow of light. It is a picture of the faithfulness of God and His mercy, setting aside His bow of judgment. In his vision of the glorious throne of God, John saw the rainbow as a sign of God's mercy (Revelation 4:3).

afteR tHe fLood

The first part of the Noahic Covenant is a promise that God will restrain His judgment. God then provides protection from the animal realm. The animal realm now becomes "red of tooth and red of claw." There aren't enough plants to sustain all the animals, so they begin to eat each other. If you were an animal, what is the easiest, biggest, fattest, slowest animal to catch? It's man! He can't run, he can't hide, and he can't dig. God says in verses 1 and 2, "I'm going to put terror between you and the animals. They are going to treat you as kings of the beasts, and they'll always run from you" (Genesis 9:1-2). And verse 3 states, "You're not going to have enough food to go around, so I'm going to let you harvest the animals and eat them."

Friends, if you want to be a vegetarian, don't make that decision on theological grounds. As Christians, animals are created for us. You catch them, kill them, fillet them, make brisket or barbecue, eat them, and thank God (I Timothy 4:3-5). Sounds like a church picnic, doesn't it?

So God first gave a promise of protection, and then of provision. In the pre-flood civilization when Cain committed murder, God made an example of him by separating him from other people. But this didn't work. Man became violent and murderous. God then instituted a new method to restrain the evil of man, human government, which is the third administration of the earth after innocence and conscience. At this point, God gave man the right, the authority, and the responsibility to discipline his own race, even in taking human life.

People sometimes ask me if I believe in capital punishment. Yes, I do. Why? Because it's taught in Romans 13. Paul said the Roman centurion "does not bear the sword for nothing. He is a minister of God who brings wrath on the one who practices evil." Capital punishment is also found throughout the Old Testament. In the Noahic Covenant, before the law was given, we read, "Whoever sheds man's blood by man his blood shall be shed" (Genesis 9:6-7). Capital punishment is instituted and ordered by God because of the dignity of man. Capital punishment is not just a New Testament teaching. It is a pre-law teaching carried on in Israel and certified by the Apostle Paul in Romans 13 as well as the Apostle Peter in I Peter 2:14. Peter, Paul, Noah, and Moses taught the appropriate use of capital punishment.

In verse 7, God commanded Noah to fill the earth and use this new institution of government to establish God's rule. "As for you, be fruitful, multiply, populate the earth, multiply abundantly in it." The flood had been a testimony of God's judgment, faithfulness, mercy, and preservation. Will mankind now submit to this God of justice and mercy and veracity who gives him the responsibility to eliminate evildoers through capital punishment? Will government work? Let's see.

The first man, Adam, ate a forbidden fruit in the Garden. When he realized he was naked in his sin, he was covered by the skin of an animal and God turned His back on sin. Now Noah gets a completely fresh start, but has man changed? "Noah became a farmer and planted a vineyard...." (Another garden!) "And he drank of the wine and he became drunk." (Another forbidden fruit!) This is the first mention in the Bible of drunkenness, and it is depicted as an evil thing. Man is not to be controlled by a substance, whether it is alcohol, peyote, or marijuana. "And he uncovered himself in the tent." (Adam became naked, and now Noah is naked.)

What had to happen to Adam when he sinned? His sin had to be atoned by the death of a substitutionary animal, then God turned his back on Adam's sin. The same thing occurred here. Verse 22 states, "And Ham, the father of Canaan, saw the nakedness of his father and told his two brothers outside."

Why did Ham tell his brothers? Because Ham was a wicked boy, and wicked men enjoy telling others when righteous men sin. In recent years, several "television preachers" admitted to—or were caught in—sexual sin. Their sins were broadcast on the front pages of all the newspapers: The *Newsweek* account wasn't called "Water Gate;" it was called "Pearly Gates."The world glories in the fall of good men and women.

Ham saw his righteous father drunk, so he ran to get his brothers. He laughed, "You've got to take a look at this!" Shem and Japheth, Noah's two other sons, took a garment (an animal skin), laid it on their shoulders, and walked backward to cover the nakedness of their father. Just as Adam was covered with the garment of an animal, so was Noah. Just as God turned his back on Adam's sin, the brothers turned their backs on their father's sin and looked away.

This is a marvelous lesson for how a child of God should respond to peer pressure. Whenever someone comes to you and wants you to glory in another person's sin, your task is the same as Shem and Japheth: Turn your back publicly and refuse to look upon it. They covered their father in respect.

God provided order under the Noahic Covenant. But there was a problem—a big problem! Sin! Noah didn't do any better than Adam. There was sin, nakedness, atonement, and forgiveness for Noah, just as there was with Adam. We have met the enemy, and he is us! Adam was a sinner; Noah was a sinner.

And look at Noah's child. He has his own version of Cain. "Noah awoke from his wine and knew what his youngest son had done to him, so he said, 'Cursed be Canaan, a servant of servants he shall be to his brothers.'" Canaan is the son of Ham. A son sinned against Noah, and a son will sin against Ham. The Canaanites are cursed here because they treat the nakedness of their father with disdain.

In the book of Leviticus, Israel goes into the land of Canaan to conquer it. Leviticus 18 shows the wickedness of the Canaanites, and the word "nakedness" is mentioned 26 times. They became as perverse as their ancient father.

In Genesis 9:26, see who receives the blessing of God. This blessing has started with Seth, it has gone through Noah, and now from Noah it will go to his son Shem. "Blessed be the

Lord, the God of Shem." The word "Shem" is the Hebrew word for "name." God is saying, "Blessed be God who will make a name for himself by Shem." But who are the Semitic people, the descendants of Shem? They are the Jews and Arabs. So now the promise of the Redeemer is going to come through a Semite, a Jew or an Arab. That's all we know at this point. Stay tuned!

construction delays

What happens to the world under the new institution of government? Do you think people will do as God instructed: fill the earth, be fruitful and multiply, sacrifice and repent before the God of mercy? Will they move to their different regions and institute the kingdom of God? Will they offer sacrifice like Adam, Abel, and Noah?

Seventy nations exist in Genesis 10. Chapter 11 shows how the nations were divided—not by the wise decision to carry out the righteous rule of God, but rather because of man's perversion.

Genesis 11 quickly sets the scene: "Now the whole earth used the same language and the same words. And it came about as they journeyed east, they found the plain, the land of Shinar, and they settled there. And they said to one another, 'Come, let us make bricks and burn them thoroughly.' And they used brick for stone and they used tar for mortar. Then they said, 'Come, let us build for ourselves a city, and a tower whose top will reach into heaven, and let us make for ourselves a name, lest we be scattered abroad over the face of the earth'" (vv. 1-4).

Here was yet another city, located in what is now Iraq. And its motto, it seems, was "*Ours* is the kingdom, and the power, and the glory forever." The tower into heaven was designed to replace God in the heart of man. That's why this city was called Babylon. "Babel" means "the gate of God." It's the renunciation of God and the enthronement of man. They proclaim in defiance and arrogance, "Let's make a kingdom and an authority and a name for ourselves. Let's replace God with ourselves. Let's not fill the earth and multiply and worship God and establish His kingdom. Let's make ourselves gods!" Now what can God do? Will He destroy the earth? He can't, because He has already made a promise that He won't. There's only one thing that can be done.

If you teach a group of small children who won't stop talking, what do you do? You have to separate them. And that's what God did to the defiant people of Babel. He turned "the gate of God" into "confusion." He split up their languages and made them into nations which couldn't communicate with each other. God divided them in order to retard the spread of evil. Man always thinks humanism will bring greatness, but instead, it yields confusion.

As the people were forced to separate, they formed the 70 nations mentioned in Genesis 10. Intermarriage led to new races and man-made religions. They obliterated the knowledge of the Redeemer in order to form their own religions.

But God still has a plan. Through the line of Shem, through Noah and Seth, comes another man, a Semite. He and his wife are both 75 years of age, past the point of bearing a child. But God makes a promise to that man: "From you I'm going to make a great nation, and from your nation a seed will come through whom the whole earth will be blessed." Even in the middle of man's evil, God still demonstrates His goodness!

Reflection/discussion questions

1. Compare the evil in the world during Noah's day with the evil in the world today:

2. Imagine being left behind as the rains came and the Ark floated away. How would you have felt and acted?

3. Imagine being on the Ark as one of only a handful of people alive on the planet. How would you have felt...

    ...about Noah?
    ...about sin?
    ...about God?

4. Describe the promise and the provision in God's covenant with Noah.

5. Describe Shem and Japheth's response to Noah's nakedness and sin. In what specific relationships or situations can you follow their example?

6. Why did God separate people at the Tower of Babel?

7. How do you think God felt as He watched people build the tower?

8. What are some results of this separation that you can see in the world today?

endnotes

1 Kidner, *Genesis*, pp. 84-84.

Chapter 7

patriarchs and promises: the birth of the nation of god

Frederick the Great of Prussia asked his chaplain, "Can you give me evidence the Bible is the Word of God?" The chaplain answered confidently, "Sir, I give you one word, Israel." That chaplain was right. The Bible contains many internal claims of its integrity. There are also a number of facts which substantiate the divine origins of the Bible, and one of these is the nation Israel.

History doesn't record any other nation which has been destroyed and then restored, and this phenomenon has happened twice to the nation of Israel! Anyone who looks at Israel can detect a divine hand on that nation. Of all the nations on the earth, Israel is the only one which was established by a divine oath. Certainly, God provides for other nations. He gives them all they need to survive. But God has committed Himself by covenant to the nation of Israel, the

Abrahamic Covenant in Genesis 12:1-3.

If I want to know the depth of a Christian's understanding about the Bible, I simply ask the question, "Do you understand the Abrahamic Covenant?" If I were to ask you what it is, or where it is, and what its relevance is to the rest of the Bible, could you give a good answer? I hope the pages of this chapter will give you a running start.

We have seen that in the Garden of Eden God created man in an innocent state, but Adam's sin resulted in the fall of humankind and the curse on the earth. After that, God promised a redeemer: "The woman's seed will crush the serpent's head" (Genesis 3:15). God instituted sacrifices which depicted His ultimate sacrifice yet to come—His Son. In the post-fall world, man lived under the requirement of conscience. That world rebelled against God and was judged. After God destroyed the world, He established government. God gave man the authority and responsibility to discipline himself and to bring about the destruction of evil men, yet at the Tower of Babel, man exalted himself as God.

Through each of these times of innocence, conscience, and government, man refused to submit to God. After all this, God established a nation of His chosen people. He didn't choose an established nation of might and power. Instead, He chose a man and woman who were old and barren. He promised to give them a baby. From the barren womb of Sarah, God gave a child called Isaac. To Isaac's barren wife, Rebekah, God gave twins, Esau and Jacob. From Jacob (later renamed "Israel"), God gave twelve sons who were the origin of the twelve tribes. This nation developed into millions of people. Israel became a nation conceived by divine power and divine grace, resting on divine veracity of the Word of God in the Abrahamic Covenant. This nation owed everything to God. But did they love Him?

aBRaHam

Genesis 11:10-26 traces the lineage of Abraham. Verse 10

tells us, "These are the records of the generations of Shem." Noah had three children: Shem, Ham, and Japheth. God promised the Redeemer, the Christ, would come from one of those sons. In Genesis 11:26, we now trace Shem's lineage to Abraham.

God's promise to Abraham in Genesis 12:1-3 signals something new. God narrows His focus from the entire world to a single nation. That nation will be the means through which the entire world will be blessed.

This passage contains three aspects of the Abrahamic Covenant which are to be repeated and reemphasized frequently. "Now the Lord said to Abraham, 'Go forth from your country, from your relatives and your father's house to the land that I will show you'" (Genesis 12:1). That's the first promise: *land*. It's fascinating to realize the Arab world has 500 times the land area of the nation of Israel. The nation of Israel is one little strip on the Mediterranean known in Abraham's day as Canaan. The Arab world, however, claims Israel has too much land. They want Israel's little strip! But God says, "I promise you, Israel, this is your land."

Verse 2 states, "I'll make you a great nation, and I'll bless you, and I'll make your name great." The promise here is for a *nation* to come. God promises an entire group of people will come from this man and his barren wife. At the end of verse 2 is a command in Hebrew: "Be a blessing." In this post-Babel world of idolatry, one little nation is a point of light.

Verse 3 tells us, "I will bless those who bless you. The one who curses you, I will curse, and in you all of the families of the earth shall be blessed." Land, nation, and also *blessing*. God promised to bless the entire world. Through a Jew, Jesus Christ, God redeemed white people, black people, red people, and yellow people through the promise of the Abrahamic Covenant.

This covenant is immutable, which means unchangeable. What activity was required of Israel under the covenant? None. It's a unilateral covenant. There are no requirements on Israel's part. God said, "I will…give land. I will…give descendants. I will...give a blessing." In Genesis 26:2-3, God repeated this covenant to Isaac: "The Lord appeared to him (Isaac) and said, 'Do not go down to Egypt, stay in the land. Sojourn in this land and I will be with you and bless you. For to you and your descendants, I will give all these lands, and I will establish the oath which I swore to your father Abraham, and I will multiply your descendants as the stars of heaven, and I will give your descendants all these lands, and by your descendants all the nations of the earth shall be blessed.'" Land, nation, and blessing—the same promise was repeated to Isaac.

In Genesis 28, Abraham's grandson Jacob flees to Ur of the Chaldees to avoid being killed by his angry brother Esau. There God appears to him in Jacob's well-known vision of a ladder from heaven. We see the same three aspects of the Abrahamic Covenant repeated to Jacob: "And behold the Lord stood above the ladder and said, 'I am the Lord, the God of your father Abraham, the God of Isaac. I will give to you and your descendants the land on which you lie. Your seed shall be like the dust of the earth, and you shall spread out to the west, east, north, and south, and in you all the earth shall be blessed'" (Genesis 28:13-14). Land, seed (or nation), and blessing.

Even though Israel sinned, God didn't forget His promise. When Israel built the golden calf after the Exodus from Egypt, God said He would wipe out every sinful person and begin all over with Moses. But Moses appealed to God: "Remember Abraham, Isaac, and Israel, thy servants to whom thou didst swear by thyself and did say to them, 'I will multiply your descendants as the stars of the heaven, and all of this land which I have spoken I will give to your descendants, and they will inherit it forever'" (Exodus 32:13). Moses appealed to the unchangeable Abrahamic Covenant: "God, you promised Abraham!"

Incidentally, the blessing was promised 500 years before God provided the Law and the Ten Commandments. Hence, salvation does not come through the Ten Commandments.

It comes through the seed of Abraham, Jesus Christ. The Abrahamic Covenant can have no additional condition. This covenant also makes the nation of Israel sacred. Paul taught that God would never, ever be finished with the nation Israel. Christ will return, judge Israel, and establish that nation again because of the Abrahamic Covenant. Paul said it like this, "If the root of the tree be holy, all of the branches that come from it are holy also" (Romans 11:16). The root of Israel's tree is Abraham, and the branches which grow from it are his nation, a nation which is holy because its origin is Abraham. That man was given an oath by God, and someday the Jewish nation will be established by God. Not every single Jew who ever lived will be saved, but someday God will establish a godly nation on that land. Sin may cloud the nation's relationship with God, but it cannot sever the bond.

This is why I am pre-millennial. I believe there will be a Second Coming just like Revelation teaches. Israel is the central nation in the book of Revelation. Jesus Christ will establish His promises to Abraham upon that nation. You and I might enjoy some of the spiritual benefits of those promises given to Israel, but the church doesn't replace Israel. God has grafted us into that "rich root of the olive tree" (Romans 11:17), but His promises still apply to His chosen nation. "The gifts and the calling of God are irrevocable" (Romans 11:29).

Chapters 12 through 50 of Genesis describe the time of promise to the patriarchs (*patri* [father] + *archs* [first] = the first fathers). Abraham is a prominent figure in New Testament theology. In the Book of Romans, Abraham is called "the father of all who believe, whether circumcised or uncircumcised" (Romans 4:12). He was saved by faith, and he is a picture of the believer in his rebirth, his life, and in his death: past, present, and future. You and I follow in the footsteps of Abraham's faith.

When I was in high school, I was part of a mouthy bunch of hooligans our civics teacher tried to keep under control. Out of the blue one day she asked us, "Who was Abraham?" Because the answer required a knowledge of Scripture somewhat above that of a philodendron, none of us had a clue! But my friend Mike took a shot and answered, "He's a prophet." The girl next to me, an academic leader of our senior class, looked at me and said, "I didn't realize Mike knew so much about the Bible." As I look back and reflect on this incident, I don't know which was funnier: the fact that Mike thought Abraham was merely a prophet, that the girl thought Mike was right, or that I thought she was so observant for pointing out Mike's biblical acumen. None of us were close to understanding who Abraham really was.

Abraham is the example of our salvation. God showed Abraham all the stars of the heavens, and Abraham believed the promises of God (Genesis 15:6). Paul used the example of Abraham to explain what faith really is: "Abraham believed in the Lord, and God reckoned it to him as righteousness" (Romans 4:3). The leader and the originator of the nation of Israel was not saved by his good works! He was saved by believing the promise of God. And because of his faith, God "reckoned" righteousness to him. To "reckon" something means that you take it out of your account and place it in the account of someone who has never earned it.

Today my son is at Ft. Riley, Kansas, in the Army Infantry. He calls home every so often, especially when he's out of money. My wife and I take money out of our account at the bank, and we tell them to "reckon" it to the account of our son. The bank takes money I earned and puts it in his account just as if he earned it. He can write checks on it just like it's his money. It is "reckoned" money. Abraham's was a "reckoned" righteousness. He is mankind's example of how to approach God.

How do you know Abraham had real faith? He demonstrated it as an example of faithful living. Fifteen years after God's promise, he took his son Isaac and put him on an altar. He was willing to put a knife in him because God said, "In Isaac shall your seed be named." Abraham believed God could raise Isaac from the dead. In James 2, that incident is used to illustrate the fact that faith without works is not the real thing. "How do you know real faith?" James asks his readers. "Because it works!" Did Abraham have real faith? Yes, he did. He's the example of faith and the example of life.

Abraham is also our example in death. Just before he died, Abraham bought a piece of land. He purchased it and was given a title deed. He buried his wife's body in that land and gave instructions for his own body to be buried there as well as his son and his grandsons. Abraham didn't want to return to the land of his birth. Even though he had never seen the nation multiply, and even though that promised child, the Redeemer through whom the earth would be blessed, had never come, Abraham believed someday these things would happen.

You and I probably are going to die in the same way father Abraham died. Our hearts are going to quit, the life support machines will flat-line, our eyes are going to flutter, and we will to pass into eternity having never seen Jesus Christ. You and I hope and believe God is true to His Word, and we will pass into eternity in heaven. We will trust in nothing but the promise of God—just like Abraham. In Hebrews 6:12, the writer encourages us to "be imitators of those who by faith and perseverance inherited the promises." This writer highlights the death of Abraham and points out that he died in faith. Abraham is the example of a true saint.

But Abraham, the example of faith, was by no means perfect. On two occasions, his fear motivated him to lie about his wife. By telling interested suitors that she was his sister, Abraham's deceit almost broke up his family. On another occasion, he became impatient with God as he waited for the promise of a son, and he fathered a child by Sarah's handmaiden, Hagar. The resulting birth of Ishmael resulted in immediate family conflict and ongoing hatred between Arabs (descendants of Ishmael) and Jews (descendants of Isaac) throughout history.

isaac and jacob

Abraham's family problems continued into the next generations. His son, Isaac, had twin sons. God had made it clear to Isaac, "The older will serve the younger" (Genesis 25:23). "Jacob [the younger] I loved, and Esau [the elder] I hated" (Malachi 1:2-3). Yet Isaac rebelled against the Word of God. Esau was a big, strong hunter, but Jacob was a boy who stayed in the kitchen. Their father, Isaac, had a "taste for game." He liked the fresh meat Esau provided from his hunts. Isaac's palate ruled over the Word of God. He tried to bless Esau even though God clearly had commanded that the blessing go to Jacob.

Jacob and his mother, Rebekah, conspired to manipulate Esau and lie to Isaac. They got what they wanted, but not without consequence. Esau threatened to kill his twin, and Jacob had to go away for 20 years. Jacob continued to have a problem with lying, deceiving, and manipulating. He struggled with God—both figuratively and literally. In a rather one-sided wrestling match, God eventually made it clear who was in control and brought Jacob to a place of yieldance. God always breaks those He chooses (Genesis 32:22-32).

joseph

Jacob had two wives and two concubines. Through them, he had twelve sons who weren't exactly the finest examples of faith and godliness! The people of the promise ultimately prove to be no better than their ancestors. The eleventh son, Joseph, was righteous, and God placed the blessing of the firstborn on him. Joseph dreamed that someday his brothers would bow down to him, but when he shared his dream with them, they weren't too impressed! They wanted to kill him, but they realized, "We can make more money out of him by selling him than by killing him." So they sold him for 20 shekels (about eight ounces) of silver. To make matters worse, they told their father Joseph had been killed by a wild animal. They sinned against God, against Joseph, and against their parents.

Yet God chose a gracious way to solve Joseph's dilemma. He converted those brothers. Famine came to Canaan and the brothers were sent away to Egypt for food. In the meantime, Joseph (through an unusual set of circumstances) had risen to prominence over the land of Egypt. He was second in command to Pharaoh himself.

When the brothers stood before Joseph seeking food, he recognized them but they didn't recognize him. Joseph is a picture of Jesus Christ, who, after mankind's rejection of Him, went to the right hand of God. God said of Christ, "Every knee shall bow to Him," and that's what Pharaoh said of Joseph. Even though his Hebrew brothers think he's dead, Joseph is alive and reigning over Gentiles. Though Christ was killed, He was raised from the dead and today rules His church.

Joseph went through several steps to reveal to his brothers the enormity of their guilt. He brought them before him, and he reminded them what they had done. They began to think about the fact that God knew how they had treated Joseph. They feared He was punishing them. Joseph blessed his brothers and gave them grain, then he sent them back home. Before he sent them away, however, he tested them. He put a silver cup in the saddlebag of the youngest brother, Benjamin, who was born of Rachel, the mother of Joseph. Rachel was the bride Jacob loved most, and Joseph incurred the jealousy of the brothers because of that special love.

On the way back to Canaan, Joseph sent his guard to surround his brothers on their camels and donkeys. He asked them, "Why have you done this? Why have you stolen from us?" One of the brothers, Judah, got down off his mount and said, "We're innocent. Check our saddlebags, and the one on whom you find that cup is a dead man." They went through the bags, and they found the hidden cup in the possession of Benjamin. Those brothers found themselves in the same position they had faced about 20 years earlier. This time, would they send Benjamin, the son of Jacob and Rachel, to his death? Or would they repent? Joseph watched. When they returned to Joseph's house, Judah got down off his mount and said, "We are guilty, both we and the one in whose possession you have found the cup. What can we say to our lord?" (Genesis 44:16) They were speechless. At that point Judah said, "This young boy is loved by his father, and if I don't bring him home, his father's gray head will go down to Sheol in sorrow." Judah repented of the grief he had brought on Jacob, and he said to Joseph, "Kill me in his place." Upon seeing their repentance, Joseph sent everyone out of the room and revealed himself to his brothers. Just as God brings people to repentance today, Joseph brought his brothers to a point where they turned from their sin and re-instituted a relationship with Joseph. Those men experienced Joseph's (and God's) forgiveness and were converted. The brothers returned to Canaan and then brought their father, Jacob, to Egypt to escape the famine. In Egypt, the few multiplied into millions. They became a great nation—just as God had promised Abraham. During the 430 years they lived in Egypt, however, the Jewish people eventually became slaves and suffered oppression. At the end of that time, God anointed Moses to lead them out of bondage to the promised land. Did God's people obey in Egypt?

the deliverer

Ezekiel 20:6-7 states, "On the day I swore to them to bring them out from the land of Egypt into the land that I have selected for them, flowing with milk and honey, which is the glory of all lands. And I said to them, 'Cast away each of you the detestable things of his eyes. Do not defy yourselves with the idols of Egypt. I am the Lord your God.'"

Verses 8-10 continue: "But they rebelled against me and were not willing to listen to me. They did not cast away the detestable things of their eyes, nor did they forsake the idols of Egypt, then I resolved to pour out my wrath on them and to accomplish my anger upon them in the land of Egypt. But I acted for the sake of my name, that it should not be profaned in the sight of the nations among whom they lived, in whose side I made myself known to them by bringing them out of the land of Egypt. So I took them out."

Even when given the promises of God, His people were still disobedient! But when disobedience resulted in groaning, bondage, servitude, oppression, and the genocide of Pharaoh killing their babies, God sent a deliverer. God used this deliverer to give His people the written law. Will these blessings encourage people to obey God? Keep reading.

Reflection/discussion questions

1. In what ways was Abraham an example of faith? What were the results?

2. In what ways did he blow it? What were the results?

3. What are some parallels between the life of Joseph and the life of Christ?

4. Do you find it odd that God used Jacob, a deceitful and conniving man, as the father of the twelve tribes of Israel? Why or why not?

5. If you were a Jew living in Israel today, how would the Abrahamic Covenant's promise of land, a nation, and blessing shape your attitude toward the frequent wars in the region, the long peace process, and the politics of the nation?

Chapter 8

tHe GIVInG
of tHe Law

After the call of Moses, God led the nation out of Egypt and miraculously through the parted Red Sea. Even as the masses of people marched through the frightful wilderness, God provided for them. They had manna to eat and water to drink every day—even if it had to come out of solid rock. On occasion, God provided quail from the wilderness. The people never hungered or thirsted. Yet in spite of God's provision, the people complained.

God's leading was clear due to the presence of a cloud by day and the fire of His glory by night. He brought the Isra-elites from the Red Sea all the way to a mountain called Sinai (which is sometimes called Mount Horeb). At this time, God gave Israel something He had given no other nation. It was the greatest blessing Israel could possess: the law. The Psalmist said, "God declares his words to Jacob, His statutes and His ordinances to Israel. He has not dealt thus with any nation. As for His ordinances, no nation hath known them. Praise the Lord!" (Psalm 147:19-20) Writing to the Romans, the apostle Paul said, "Then what advantage has the Jew? Great in every respect. First of all, they were entrusted with the oracles of God" (Romans 3:2).

commandments. . . and more

In the book of Exodus, God gave the law which consisted of three things: the moral law, the hygienic law, and ceremonial law. The moral law taught the holiness of God. God never thought or pretended the nation of Israel would keep His Word, so He instituted ceremonial law in the tabernacle and the sacrifices of the priesthood to show how people could approach God in spite of violations of the law. The shedding of blood in sacrifices was their means of forgiveness. Ritual, hygienic law prescribed clean bodies, clean homes, clean clothing, and a clean diet. Israel was to be a holy and clean nation, separate from all other nations. That was Israel's privilege of having God's law.

Moses came down from the mountain and found the nation in idolatry, worshipping an idol, a golden calf. He had been gone only forty days before they had an orgy!

God was furious and again threatened to destroy the nation. But Moses bowed down before Him and said (in a statement typical of Christ), "God, take my life! Don't take them. Kill me, but let them live!" Of course, God didn't expect Moses to die for Israel. Only one man would ever give His life for a people: not Moses, not Elijah, not David—just Jesus Christ. In His mercy, God allowed the nation to continue to exist because of Moses' intercession.

The book of Exodus explained how the tabernacle should be constructed. The next book is Leviticus, the place where most of us quit when we're trying to read through our Bibles! Here we come to the "pots and pans" part of the Old Testament. These directives are written to the Levites, who were to serve as the priests of Israel.

Make a note regarding the order of Scripture: As soon as the Law is given (in Exodus), the next book (Leviticus) describes how to deal with violations of the Law. Some people think they will be righteous by keeping the Ten Commandments, but God knew (and knows) we cannot follow the commandments. That's why Leviticus follows Exodus. After God demands perfection in our hearts and our actions, He then establishes forgiveness for our inability—and our unwillingness—to follow these perfect demands.

In Leviticus 26, we see the ratification of the Old Testament covenant. The head of an estate made a pact with his servants, "If you obey me, I will protect you. If you serve me, I'll provide for you. Fight my battles, and I'll give you protection, food, and shelter." This was a two-way conditional cove-nant. The flip side was, of course, that if you didn't do what you were told, then the master was under no obligation to provide for you and protect you. In the law, God made this kind of covenant with Israel. Leviticus 26 is the ratification of that covenant to that particular generation. In verse 3, God promised, "If you will walk in my statutes and keep my commandments so as to carry them out, then I shall give you rains." But later, in verse 14, "If you do not obey me and do not carry out all these commandments, I in turn, will do this to you: I will bring upon you sudden terror, wasting diseases and fever that will destroy your sight and drain away your life." God continued to describe more suffering which would result from disobedience, but you get the idea!

In the next book, Numbers, God took a census of the nation to help the people see how He had kept His promise to Abraham to make them a great nation. At that time they totaled over two million people. He brought them to the very edge of the land He had promised them, and Moses sent in twelve spies to check out the Promised Land. The spies saw that the land was incredibly fruitful, just like God said it was. In fact, they put a single cluster of grapes on a pole to carry between them because it was so heavy! And

yet ten of the spies were afraid to trust God. They reported
that the Canaanites would destroy them. By this time, God
was disgusted with their unbelief. They had seen and tasted
the promise, but still they refused to believe. Therefore, he
decreed that everyone over 20 years old would die in the
wilderness. Their children would be given the land instead.
Again, through the mouths of infants and nursing babes, God
would establish strength.

The people wandered in the wilderness for 40 years without actually going anywhere! It was simply the prescribed
period of time for the old, complaining generation to
die and be replaced by a more faithful generation. Then God
provided a second law, a *duet nomas* (or *nomos*),
to the new generation. In chapters 1-11, He reiterated His
goodness to Israel even though they had violated His clear
instructions. They rebelled against Him at Sinai, and they
sinned against Him at Kadesh Barnea by refusing to occupy
the Promised Land, but He had still been good to them. In
chapters 12-26, He enumerated the law to that younger
generation. Deuteronomy 28:1 says, "And it shall be, if you
will diligently obey the Lord your God, being careful to do
all these commandments which I command you today, the
Lord your God will set you high above the nations." Verse 15
reminds them, "And it will come about if you will not obey the
Lord your God to observe His statutes and commands which
I charge you today that all these curses shall come upon you."
Then He delineates another list of the tragic results of sin.
Deuteronomy 28 is a second ratification of God's two-way,
conditional covenant to the new generation.

tHe puRpose of tHe Law

Why was the law given? The purpose of the law was
something like the role of a nanny. What's the function of a
nanny? To take care of a child as long as he remains a child,
and to help him grow until he doesn't need a nanny anymore.
We give rules and guidelines to children until they are mature

and responsible enough to be free.

The prophet Jeremiah foretold of a day when God would institute a New Covenant which was internal instead of external. Jeremiah wrote, "Someday, God says, 'I will make a new covenant with the nation Israel, not like the covenant I made with their fathers when I took them by the hand to lead them out of the land of Egypt. This is the covenant that I will make with them in that day. I'll put my law on their hearts. On their minds, I will write it. I'll be their God, and they'll be My people'" (Jeremiah 31:31-33). The law was a temporary guide until the One came who offered life.

Here are seven wonderful purposes the law served during the infancy of the nation of Israel:

1. The will of God was revealed in the law. There was no ambiguity because the law taught people how to treat their parents, neighbors, and God. Paul said it was "holy, righteous, and good" (Romans 7:12).

2. The law protected the nation from evil men. It severely punished evildoers but gave godly people nothing to fear. "The law is not made for a righteous man but for those who are lawless and rebellious. . ." (I Timothy 1:9).

3. The law enabled the nation to enjoy the promises God made to Abraham. By the nation's obedience, the unique blessings of God were granted to Israel.

4. The law separated Israel from heathen people. Ceremonial and moral law kept God's chosen nation unique.

5. The ceremonies of the law educated the nation. Blood atonement, instituted in the law, helped Jewish people understand the importance of trusting in the shed blood of a substitute, and ultimately, a Redeemer.

Christianity, then, is actually the fulfillment of ortho-
dox, biblical Judaism. When John the Baptist said,
"Behold the Lamb of God that takes away the sin of
the world," the Jewish people understood what that
meant, or they should have, because they had seen
hundreds of lambs slaughtered as sacrifices for sin.

6. The law restricted the nation during its infancy, just
    as a parent puts restrictions on a child. When a Jewish
    boy has his Bar Mitzvah and receives the benefits of
    sonship, he is given freedom and responsibility as a
    member of the adult community. Israel was put under
    law until the nation had its Bar Mitzvah in Jesus Christ.
    Jesus died to free people from the law so they could
    live in maturity under grace (Galatians 4:1-7).

7. The major purpose of the law, according to Romans
    7, was to remove ambiguity about guilt. It was a
    mirror to reflect the sins. A mirror does not make you
    clean, but it removes any doubt about the need for
    cleansing.

I remember a recent service my church held at a nearby
prison. The inmates did not appear to be a model audience.
My opening statement was, "If a great man came into this
room, you would all stand up. If Jesus Christ came into this
room, you would all bow down because He said He was
God." I explained the gospel and pointed out that heaven is
a free gift which is not earned or deserved. My second point
was that the reason heaven is free is that man has no buying
power. Man has sinned against the law of God.
My listeners became the quietest audience I've ever had
when I began to recite the law of God. "Thou shalt not kill.
Thou shalt not steal. Thou shalt love thy neighbor as thyself. Thou shalt not raise your voice against your father and
mother." I said, "Ladies and gentlemen, if you have violated
any one of those, you must perish in hell." Stone silence. Then

I said, "But I have some good news! Somebody else has born the talon of the law." Then I told them about the Son of God. I don't know how they responded back in their cells, but they cheered right then. I had never been applauded after a gospel message, but that was the response of this group. The law of God revealed their guilt and showed them their need for a Savior.

The law does not replace the Abrahamic Covenant. It was a temporary covenant instituted by God to protect and educate the nation until the coming of the seed God had promised to Abraham. If you say you are going to heaven because you have kept the Ten Commandments, you have violated the very reason the commandments were given. No human being—except one—could possibly keep them. We fail. We sin. Our hearts are desperately wicked. We need a Savior. That's why Leviticus follows Exodus. That's why the tabernacle and the sacrifices follow Sinai. That's why the New Covenant follows the old. Divine law leads us from Sinai to Calvary so we might be saved by intercession.

from moses to jesus

We're going to move ahead quickly to the birth of Jesus, but it's a shame to skip over all the sacred stories that fill the rest of the Old Testament. Israel was a nation that should have died in Egypt, but God had mercy. They should have died at Sinai, but God was again merciful. You would think they would have then learned to honor His law in humble thankfulness. Sadly, they didn't. Look at how Israel fared under God's law.

Under Joshua's leadership, they conquered the Promised Land and seized the land of Canaan. But in no time "a generation arose which did not know God nor the things which He had done for Israel. They forsook God and served idols" (Judges 2:10-11). God called judges to put them back on the right track. Each successive judgment proved to be more harsh. The book of Judges records cycles of sin, judgment, crying out, deliverance, blessing, and sin again.

Eventually the nation went to Samuel (the last judge) and said, "We don't want a judge. We want to be like the other nations. We want a king to fight our battles" (I Samuel 8). God responded to their request, and the nation seemed to improve under the successive reigns of Saul, David, and Solomon. In this brief time, God made a covenant that His Messiah would come through David (II Samuel 7). God is quick to bless, and He is slow to anger. But the sins of these leaders eventually outweighed their positive influences.

David committed adultery with Bathsheba and murdered her husband and brought heartache to the nation. Their second child, Solomon, started off well as king. But he tried to expand his empire by marrying the daughters of pagan kings to form alliances. He eventually turned away and worshiped their gods. God was so angry He told Solomon He would tear the kingdom from his descendants.

Solomon's son was Rehoboam. And almost immediately after he became king, the kingdom split. The northern kingdom rebelled against Rehoboam and followed a wicked man named Jeroboam. In time, the kingdom of Israel became so wicked that through idolatry, perversion, and murder, God allowed them to be wiped from the face of the earth by the Assyrian empire. The kingdom of the south, under the Judean/ Davidic kings, also became wicked. They were defeated by the Babylonians and taken into exile for 70 years. During that time, the majority of the old generation died.

During the period of exile under Babylon and Persia, we see some of the Bible's greatest stories of courage.

Daniel, Shadrach, Meshach, Abednego, Ezra, Nehemiah, Esther, and Mordecai. Finally, the people returned to their homeland and restored the nation.

Conquest. Judges. Monarchy. Division. Exile. And finally, return.

During the period of time between the Old and New Testaments, Israel fell to the Greeks, who were in turn conquered by the Romans. By the time of Christ's birth, an

Edomite named Herod controlled the northern part of the nation. A Roman named Pontius Pilate controlled Jerusalem. The once great and glorious nation of Israel was only a little flicker of what it had been. It had violated the law and suffered the consequences over and over again. Just like those who came before them, the nation refused to keep God's law. God said, "If you won't, I won't." They didn't, and He didn't. He judged them, but in mercy He brought them back to the land of promise because of His promises to Abraham and David.

At this point in Israel's history, things looked bleak. But one night, some shepherds were working outside Bethlehem in a field called "The Tower of the Flock." These shepherds raised lambs which were used for sacrifices in Jerusalem. They watched their flocks by night, and when an infant lamb was born, they wrapped it to protect it. On this special night, these simple men saw the dramatic watershed in God's eternal plan.

Reflection/discussion questions

1. What is the relationship between the law and the sacrifices?

2. How does understanding the purpose of the law affect your response to it?

3. Describe the differences between the Mosaic Covenant and the Abrahamic Covenant.

4. How was the outworking of the Mosaic Covenant visible during the periods of conquest and the judges? How was the outworking of the Abrahamic Covenant visible during the periods of conquest and the judges?

Chapter 9

THE COMING OF THE KING
...and HIS REJECTION

For many people, understanding the life of Christ is like playing a game of Scrabble. They recognize the letters, but they have a hard time arranging them into something meaningful. They know something about Christ's death on the cross, the resurrection, and a parable here and there, but they can't put Jesus' life together. They don't follow the sequence of Christ's presentation of Himself to Israel, His rejection by the Jews, His mission to the Gentiles, and the promise of His return to establish Israel according to God's covenant. They just don't see the scope of the program of God. Matthew's gospel presents Christ's life to show his readers "who is the king and where is the kingdom."

The gospel of Matthew begins, "The book of the genealogy of Jesus Christ, son of David, son of Abraham." This is the title of the Messiah in the Old Testament. This man

Jesus is the "Son of David" and the chosen seed of Abraham. In Christ's genealogy, we find some intriguing people: four Gentile women, including Ruth the Moabite; Rahab the harlot; Tamar, who committed incest with Judah; and Bathsheba, who committed adultery with David. In the genealogy of Jesus, we see the incredible breadth of God's mercies. We see the types of people He will receive into His family: the lowly of Israel, as well as the lowly of the Gentiles.

jesus' eaRLY yeaRs

The two accounts of the conception of Jesus are found in Matthew and Luke. These passages state clearly He was born of a virgin. Liberal theologians debate the virgin birth, but look at the evidence: Mary said she was a virgin; Joseph thought she was a virgin; the angel said she was a virgin; God stated emphatically that she was a virgin; and Matthew and Luke taught she was a virgin. These statements are primary resource material. Isaiah prophesied, "A virgin will be with child, and His name will be Immanuel, God with us" (Isaiah 7:14). Jesus Christ was born of a virgin, but not because God is opposed to sex. Sexuality and the tools of reproduction were created at the very origin in Genesis. And Mary's virginity didn't contribute at all to the holiness of Jesus. His holiness was His eternal nature as the Son of God.

Jesus was born of a virgin because there was no need of a human father. Jesus didn't find His origin in a male and a female. He eternally existed as the Son of God. His conception was not the origin of man. It was the incarnation of that Divine Person. "Incarnate" means "in the flesh." Mary didn't provide an origin for His deity, but she provided the means for deity to unite with humanity. A human father simply was not needed. Mary's virginity signaled the indisputable evidence that Jesus was Immanuel, God with us. He was not "conceived in sin or brought forth in iniquity" (Psalm 51:5). He does not stand in the line of

Adam in his condemnation and fall. Jesus is substantially different, even though He was very much a man.

Throughout the Old Testament, God's presence is associated with a radiance known as the *shekinah glory*. As the prophet Ezekiel spoke of the coming Babylonian destruction, he saw a vision of the glory of God in the temple. But then the shekinah glory departed the nation through the eastern gate (Ezekiel 9-10). That glory was not seen again until Matthew 2 when the visible presence of God among His people again appeared in the baby in the manger. When the glory appeared, it was a bold declaration to Israel that God was present. It rested over the cradle of a babe, Christ the Lord. Immanuel, God with us.

This glory revealed Christ's deity. The wise men asked, "Where is He that is born king of the Jews that we might worship Him?" The worship by the wise men from the east began the Gentiles' reception of this Jewish Messiah. The humble shepherds were the first of the Jews to receive Him. He didn't come in majesty. He came in a manger. To believe in Him, we must humble ourselves. That is why He is a stumbling block to the self-righteous and foolishness to the proud.

But the political King of Israel, Herod, tried to kill Him. At His birth, children were murdered and mothers wept. The two worst events in the nation's history were their captivity in Egypt and the deportation to Babylon. When Herod threatened to kill Jesus, Mary and Joseph took the boy to Egypt. Matthew 1:15 reads, "This was what was spoken by the prophet, 'Out of Egypt did I call my son.'" Matthew recalled that text from Hosea about Israel coming out of the Exodus, and he saw that it applied to Jesus Christ who was exiled in Egypt. Jesus experienced what the Jewish people had already experienced: both were exiles in Egypt.

When Israel was carried off to Babylon, Ramah was the little city outside Jerusalem from which the Jews were deported. Jeremiah wrote: "A voice is heard in Ramah, weeping and great mourning, Rachel weeping for her children and refusing to be comforted, because they are no more" (Matthew 2:18). There was weeping because the men of Israel had died, and the remnant of Israel was going into exile. Years later there was again weeping when Jesus was forced out of his country and children died. Matthew pointed out that even in His birth, Jesus Christ is identified with the people in their suffering. He experienced the same tragedies the nation experienced, the exodus and the exile. "He had to be made like His brethren in all things" (Hebrews 2:17).

Matthew doesn't talk about 30 years of Jesus' life. Israel was unaware of His true identity during those years. He lived a simple life as a carpenter's helper. Matthew stated, "He resided in the city of Nazareth that what was spoken through the prophets might be fulfilled, 'He shall be called a Nazarene'" (Matthew 2:23). The summation of the prophets' teaching about the Messiah was that He would be a Nazarene. A Nazarite, in both the Old and New Testament times, was a lowly person. Nazareth was a city in the far north in the land of the tribe of Naphtali. The residents were so far north they seldom traveled south to worship in Jerusalem. Nazarenes even had a different dialect than other Jews. Nazareth was a crossroad for Gentile commerce, and Rome established a military garrison in the town. An old saying of the time said, "If you want to be holy, live in Jerusalem. If you want to be wealthy, live in Nazareth." When Jesus was announced by Philip, "We have found Him, Jesus of Nazareth," Nathanael's response was, "Can any good thing come out of Nazareth?" (John 1:45) So, when Matthew wrote, "He shall be called a Nazarene," all of the Jews to whom this is written understood. Jesus cultural standing was lowly and despised.

Matthew 3 describes the forerunner of the Messiah, John the Baptist. When a king planned to enter a city, a forerunner went before him to raise up the low spots and bring down the high ones. The forerunner made the place level before the king. John saw himself as the fulfillment of Isaiah's prophecy (Isaiah 40:3-4). The last statement in the book of Malachi, the final book of the Old Testament is, "The next voice that you will hear will be Elijah," and "he will turn the hearts of the fathers back to the children and the hearts of the children to the fathers" (Malachi 4:5-6). The forerunner for the Messiah, then, would be a prophet just like Elijah, in power and in majesty, calling the nation to repentance. He would restore the children of Israel back to the faith of Abraham and to the Jewish fathers. He would bring them back to "that old-time religion" of repentance and obedience.

In Matthew 3:4, we see that John the Baptist looked, dressed, and ate like Elijah. In verses 7 through 9, he also preached like him. John came to the nation of Israel, and he proclaimed, "Repent!" He said, "Don't think there's any blessing just because you're a Jew! God can raise up Jews from these rocks!" He said, "Get your heart right." That message wasn't new. It was preached by Isaiah, Hosea, Micah, Jeremiah, and Ezekiel. John simply fulfilled Malachi's prophecy by calling the children back to the faith of the fathers.

And as soon as John the Baptist proclaimed his message of a coming Messiah, Jesus began His public ministry. First the forerunner; then the king.

John's baptism of Jesus is described in Matthew 3:13-17. John didn't want to baptize Jesus because he didn't see himself as worthy. But Jesus' response was, "Permit it at this time, for in this way it is fitting for us to fulfill all righteousness." What does this mean? Throughout His life, Jesus Christ perfectly obeyed God's commandments. He was a righteous Jew. He kept the feasts, the fast days, and the day of atonement—even those He didn't have to. (He was already completely sinless and holy.) He had no need to be down at the Jordan River being baptized. Yet Jesus said "it is fitting" to do so.

When John baptized Jesus, two amazing things happened. First, the heavens were opened, and the Spirit of God descended upon Jesus as a dove. Just as Noah's dove was sent out of the ark to find life, the Spirit of God came down like a dove and rested on Jesus, signifying He was clean. The dove didn't light on John the Baptist or the Pharisees, but rather on this Man who came up from the water because He was the Holy One of God.

Then, God the Father spoke from heaven. In Psalm 2, a Messianic Psalm, God says of the Messiah, "This is my son." In Isaiah 42:1, God said of the Messiah, "Behold My servant, in whom My soul delights." At Jesus' baptism, God's statement combined the two concepts—the deity of His Son (Psalm 2) and the humanity of His Son, the perfect servant (Isaiah 42).

With everything taking place at Jesus' baptism, we should have no doubt as to Jesus' identity. John the Baptist said to Israel, "Pay attention! This is the Messiah!" God the Father said, "This is My Son in whom I am well pleased." The Holy Spirit said (symbolically), "This is Him." These were three, big, neon signs flashing, "This is the One! Don't miss Him!" He is divinely qualified to be the Messiah.

When Jews read this gospel, they are often overwhelmed by these statements. The very outset of Matthew's gospel proclaims clearly, "This is the Messiah. This Jesus is virgin born. The glory is upon Him; He is God! Worship the King."

Immediately after Jesus' baptism, Satan tempted Him to assert His independence and refuse to submit to the will of God (Matthew 4). In all three temptations, Jesus responded with a quotation from the Book of Deuteronomy. He refused to assert His independence. He was perfectly obedient. Jesus' obedience was consistently demonstrated over the next three years and culminated in the Garden of Gethsemane when He faced the specter of the cross. Even then, He uttered, "Not my will, but thine be done." Jesus did what Adam refused to do: He submitted. He is morally qualified to be the Messiah.

tHe seRmon on tHe mount

Chapters 5, 6, and 7 of Matthew introduce the teaching of this Messiah in an oration called the Sermon on the Mount. At this time, Israel believed people went to heaven by the meticulous, fastidious keeping of Old Testament edicts. Heaven, they believed, had to be earned. But in this sermon,

Jesus presented quite a different argument concerning divine righteousness and the characteristics of people who are rightly related to God.

He began with the Beatitudes—moral principles which were connected with entering "the kingdom of heaven." Jesus taught that a saved man is not someone who earns the righteousness of God and pronounces himself perfect, but rather one who is "poor in spirit," who "mourns" about his condition. He is "gentle" (or meek). He has no moral pride and no personal righteousness to appeal to. Instead, he "hungers" for the righteousness of God. His life is then marked by "mercy" (or love) and "purity" (or holiness). He becomes a "peacemaker" as he brings others to find peace in God, and he is willing to "suffer for the sake of righteousness." He is willing to die for his faith. These are the characteristics of a humble person who is responsive to the grace, goodness, and greatness of God.

You don't become righteous by being good. Instead, you are righteous because you are hungry for what you don't have. That hunger is brought on by the recognition of your own poverty. The way you can tell that you are righteous is that you genuinely love others, you have moral purity, and you are willing to hold to your faith even to the point of martyrdom. That's a righteous man or woman!

As Jesus continued His sermon, He showed His listeners a proper interpretation of the Ten Commandments. The purpose of the Ten Commandments was not to serve as rungs on a ladder leading to heaven. Just the opposite: The commandments revealed evil and sin. People thought the commandment, "Don't commit adultery" meant only "Don't sleep with another man's wife." But Jesus gave its proper meaning: "I'm telling you, if you look at a woman in lust, you've violated this commandment." He continued, "You thought the law said, 'Don't murder.' But I'm saying, 'Don't even get angry.' You thought it said, 'Don't take God's name in vain.' But I'm saying, 'Don't even give an oath if you can't keep it.'"

Jesus told people (in Matthew 6:1-18) that fasting, tithing, and praying should not be done just so others can see because true religious life must be practiced in private for God to reward. He challenged people (Matthew 6:19-34) to live for divine treasures, not earthly ones, and to seek the righteousness of God instead of worldly delights. He told leaders to be humble and practice what they preached.

demonstrating the truth

To back up His powerful words, Jesus demonstrated His power in another way—His miracles. Matthew chapters 8 and 9 contain ten miracles which clearly demonstrate the deity of Christ. The miracles are over disease, demons, death, and the powers of nature.

The first miracle was typical: Jesus healed a leper. But after the miraculous healing, He told the man to go show a priest (rather than make a big scene to the surrounding multitudes). Have you ever wondered why Jesus Christ told some people not to tell anyone about a miracle they experienced? Because miracles in the Bible were not primarily acts of compassion. The purpose of miracles was to authenticate the divine messenger of law, prophecy, and grace. This had been true of Moses and Elijah, as well as Jesus.

How did the Jews respond? They rejected Him. "The Pharisees were saying, 'He cast out demons by the ruler of demons'" (Matthew 9:34). Jesus hurt for His people: "Seeing the multitudes, He felt compassion for them because they were distressed and downcast like sheep without a shepherd" (Matthew 9:36). The Pharisees, the Sadducees, the scribes, and the Herodians were meant to be the spiritual leaders of Israel, but they failed. They distorted the Word of God by their own self-righteous teaching. They used the nation for their own wealth and prestige; they left the people without a shepherd (Matthew 9:36). Just as Ezekiel had prophesied hundreds of years earlier, God Himself would be the shepherd of Israel (Ezekiel 34:11-12).

start spreading the news!

After noting the lack of spiritual leaders and telling the disciples to pray that God would send workers, Jesus informs them, "Fellows, I've got good news. God has answered your prayers. The news is, you're the answer." (Be careful what you pray!) Matthew writes, "Having summoned the twelve disciples, He gave them authority over the unclean spirits and cast them out to heal every kind of disease" (Matthew 10:1).

Jesus sent the twelve out as messengers of the King, proclaiming Him to the entire nation. Through these men, the nation saw miracles like never before. These miracles were to signify that the Messiah had come! The people should listen to His preaching! The priests, scribes, and all the rest should humble themselves.

Jesus revealed a marvelous promise in Matthew 10:40-42. He said, "Anyone who receives a prophet receives a prophet's reward. Anyone who receives a righteous man will receive a righteous man's reward. And anyone who gives you even a cup of water shall not lose his reward." In these statements, Jesus Christ cast his twelve disciples in the line of the prophets and righteous men. They were the anointed messengers of God Himself. How did the nation respond?

Chapters 11 and 12 of Matthew are central to understanding the plan of God. John the Baptist was in prison and sent word to Jesus. John wasn't weak; he lacked knowledge of the complete ministry of Jesus. He wanted to know, "Are you the expected one, the Messiah, or shall we look for someone else?" (Matthew 11:3) Jesus didn't answer the question directly. Instead, He bolstered John's faith by telling the messenger, "Go tell John this is what I'm doing: The blind see, the lame walk..." (Matthew 11:4-5). His reference to a prophecy from Isaiah meant: "I am the Messiah, and that's all you need to know."

This is the way God often deals with our questions as well. Our knowledge of God, like John's, is incomplete. But rather than address the lack of knowledge, Jesus affirms that,

"I am God. You can trust Me." When we go through hard times, God may not always provide answers, but He points to His sovereignty and goodness. He says, "I am God, and I don't make mistakes. You can trust me. Just wait and see."

Jesus publicly affirmed John the Baptist (Matthew 11:7). John's problem was not his heart; it was merely his lack of light and New Testament revelation. Jesus said, "Truly, among women there is not one born greater than John the Baptist. But he that is least in the kingdom of heaven is greater than John" (Matthew 11:11). The greatness Jesus referred to wasn't in morality or courage, but in greater understanding.

If you are a new Christian who has trusted Christ, you are greater in knowledge than John the Baptist. You understand things that John the Baptist didn't understand. He didn't understand the purpose of the rejection of Messiah like you understand it. The problem with John was not his heart but his enlightenment.

Jesus told Israel that their problem was rebellion against the Word of God. "From the days of John the Baptist until now, the kingdom of heaven suffers violence, and violent men take it by force" (Matthew 11:12), which means that men would not submit to the king's edict. Jesus told the religious leaders that John stood in the line of Moses and the prophets (Matthew 11:13). He was the divine, Elijah-like messenger. But instead of submitting to the preaching of John, they rejected him.

In Matthew 11:25-30, Jesus then shared a very important principle: Spiritual truth may be hidden from those who consider themselves wise and intelligent, yet revealed to "babes." Many of the leaders of the nation were not going to understand His teachings or His plan. Yet the disciples, the women who supported Him, and faithful Gentiles would enter the kingdom of heaven. They knew they were not righteous, but they accepted the Messiah like children would accept Him. Jesus' invitation was to all of them: "Come unto me all that are weary and heavy laden, and I will give you rest" (v. 28). The rejection of Jesus by the leaders was gathering speed. Only the lowly continued to receive Him.

responding to jesus

The religious leaders were looking for any opportunity to criticize Jesus, so when His disciples picked some grain on the Sabbath, the Pharisees were quick to challenge Him (Matthew 12:1-2). Jesus responded that it had been permissible for David and his companions to exceed the letter of the law because they had been on a divine mission. Also, priests serve on the Sabbath, so they obviously don't live by the letter of the law. Jesus, like David, is a king, and He, like the priests, must serve. He then stated something even more amazing: Jesus claimed to be the Lord of the Sabbath! (Matthew 12:8) That meant He is God, the Creator. In response to the condemnation of the Pharisees, Jesus said, in essence, "I make the rules just as I made the Sabbath."

One time, President Ronald Reagan gave a speech and someone interrupted him, asking for a chance to talk. Reagan told the man, "It's my banquet. I'll talk all I want. I paid for it!" In the same way, Jesus claimed the right to eat on the Sabbath because He created it.

Jesus further angered the religious leaders when He healed a man's shriveled hand—still on the Sabbath. Michelangelo's painting of the Sistine Chapel ceiling suggests that when Adam was created, his first instinctive move was to reach his hand out to his Creator. To demonstrate His deity, Jesus told this man, "Stretch out your hand" (Matthew 12:13). Jesus healed his hand, and the man was made new.

How should the leaders have responded to Jesus' powerful act of kindness? They should have fallen on their faces! Instead, they discussed how they might kill Him! Jesus knew their thoughts and their plans. He withdrew from that place and warned the twelve not to make Him known. But His very next encounter with the Pharisees only intensified the conflict between them. A man was brought to Jesus who was the perfect picture of Israel—demon possessed, blind, and dumb. Jesus healed this man. After hearing the preaching of Jesus and seeing His miracles, the people of Israel had a choice to make. Some expressed belief, but many concluded His power to cast out demons came from Beelzebub, the ruler of demons. They attributed the work of the Spirit of God to the devil!

The leaders had crossed the line! Jesus explained that it was an unpardonable sin to blaspheme and reject God. Israel knew there was no sacrifice that would "undo" blasphemy in the Old Testament. The punishment was death by execution. The leaders were now guilty of that sin. They had not merely disbelieved God; they had attributed His marvelous and miraculous work to the devil.

At that pivotal moment, Jesus turned from Israel and turned to the Gentiles. His invitation to enter the kingdom of God reached out to the Germans and the Norwegians, the Scandinavians and the Africans, the Irishmen and the Scots, the Asians and the Australians, the Tasmanians and the Pygmies—and you and me. Jesus came to the Jewish nation, but they rejected Him. So He turned to the nations. "He came to His own, and His own received Him not. But whoever received Him, to them He gave the power to become children of God" (John 1:11-12).

The shadow of the cross begins to rise in the narrative. "While He was still speaking to the multitudes, behold his mother and brothers were standing outside to speak to him. And someone said to Him, 'Behold your mother and your brothers are standing outside to speak to you.' And He answered the one who was telling him and said, 'Who is my mother and who are my brothers?' and stretching out His hand to the disciples, those seated at His feet" (Matthew 12:46-50). Jesus made it clear that from then on, "Whoever does the will of my Father who is in heaven, he is my brother and sister and mother."

Do you see what has happened so far in the life of Jesus? The kingdom was offered, but it was rejected as God was blasphemed. As a result, Jesus withdrew and began to spend

His time with a small remnant of Jews who were willing to believe in spite of the advice and attitudes of their religious leaders. He began to reach out to people like us to bring us into His kingdom.

The next chapter will tell you more about God's king-dom—if you have the spiritual discernment to detect the wonderful truths hidden from others in Jesus' parables.

Reflection/discussion questions

1. Is the virgin birth important to your personal faith in Christ? Why or why not?

2. How do you think you would have responded to John the Baptist and his message of repentance? Explain.

3. Imagine yourself as a Jewish person listening to Jesus. What aspects of His life and His message would have made sense to you? Why? What would have confused you? Why?

4. What is the purpose of miracles? Are miracles valid today? Why or why not?

5. If you had been one of the disciples, how would you have responded to people's rejection of Jesus?

Chapter 10

THE KING'S NEW PROGRAM: THE CHURCH

A number of years ago, one of the pastors at my church studied Hebrew with a rabbi. He asked the rabbi why he couldn't believe Jesus is the Messiah. The rabbi answered, "If Jesus is the king, where is the kingdom? The Bible teaches the Messiah will rule from Jerusalem, and that city will be the joy of the earth. That has not happened."

How would you answer this rabbi if he handed you his Old Testament and said, "Show me the church in the Holy Bible"? The fact is, it's not there. You might point to the prophecies of the death of Christ or a few other passages. But from the Old Testament, you couldn't show him the church age in which an absent Messiah loves and directs His people in a hostile world, where genuine and false believers grow up side by side, and where God will do nothing about it until a final day of judgment. The church is a New Testament truth.

That idea simply isn't explained in the Old Testament. That's why Jesus and Paul called the church "the mystery."

Matthew 13 connects the Messiah with the New Testament church. Chapter 13 explains the authority of Christ in the form of seven parables—stories which require spiritual discernment on the part of the hearer before they can be understood. A darkness had fallen on Israel's understanding, so Jesus used parables as a form of judgment of the nation and to teach His followers. He turned to the twelve and told them they had been selected to understand "the mystery" of the kingdom of heaven.

The term "mystery" needed no explanation. In that day, a mystery was similar to the secret rites (handshakes, etc.) in today's sororities and fraternities, secrets which "outsiders" aren't allowed to know. A "mystery" meant someone had inside knowledge through divine revelation which had not been revealed in the Old Testament.

When asked why He spoke in parables, Jesus replied, "Because the nation has been darkened" (Matthew 13:14-15). Jesus promised to give His faithful followers knowledge of His plan and His program which had not been spelled out in the Old Testament. Those who opposed Jesus were "darkened"; they didn't understand Him. This strange new concept of Jew and Gentile together in one body, the church, was a mystery to them. Yet by relating these parables in his gospel, Matthew validated the idea of the church to the Jews of the first century. The parables were prophetic of what was to come. In the sovereign plan of God, the church was established in response to Israel's rejection of the Messiah.

tHe paRaBLe of tHe soWeR

The seven parables in Matthew 13 are a walk through the church age. The first parable (vv. 3-23) is about a sower who throws out seed, the "message of the kingdom." This seed falls on different types of ground. The birds (symbolizing Satan) snatch up one portion of the seed before it can even take root. Another portion falls on hard ground. It takes root, but never matures. This is a picture of people who initially respond to Christ, yet never develop because they are sown in shallow soil. A third portion of seed is choked out by weeds and thorns (other "worries of this life"), and it bears no fruit. The last seed falls on ground which is cultivated. It takes root and grows, bearing 30, 60, or 100 times its original amount.

Why is this first parable important? It teaches about the wide proclamation of the kingdom, the church. The message is to everyone—good guys and bad guys, false ones and righteous ones. Time will show who are the true believers. When persecution arises, false believers fall away. Others will forsake Christ to pursue other things, such as riches and worldly recognition. But some follow Christ and become a blessing to many others.

tHe wHeat and tHe taRes

The next parable (vv. 24-30) describes the corruption of the kingdom. Jesus said, "The kingdom of heaven is like a man who sowed good seed in his field. But while everyone was sleeping, his enemy came and sowed weeds [tares] among the wheat, and went away." A tare is not wheat, but it looks similar. It's called "darnel," and it doesn't bear good fruit. The fruit it bears is toxic, just like a false Christian's life. Some people sing hymns, read the Bible, and even have clever Christian bumper stickers, but they don't bear truth or model a godly life. They are sowed, Jesus said, "by the enemy." They are Satan's kids in sheep's clothing.

The servants asked, "Do you want us to go and pull them up?" But the owner knew better. He knew that the roots of tares and wheat are intertwined beneath the soil. He gave instructions for the wheat and tares to grow together. He knew the day would come when they both would be gathered. At that point it would be simple enough to separate the wheat from the worthless tares. The good wheat would be preserved, but the weeds would be burned. It may appear that God doesn't notice. But a day is appointed when the false believers will stand before God. Judgment will come, and the wicked will be exposed.

the mustard seed

A mustard seed (vv. 31-32) is the smallest of all seeds, yet it grows to be the largest plant in the garden. The church started small, with only a few faithful men and women. Yet it rapidly grew from Jerusalem all the way to Rome and beyond. Today, you are one of millions who worship Jesus throughout the world. This parable, then, speaks of the expansion of the kingdom.

Matthew 13:32 says of the mustard plant, "Birds of the air will nest in its branches." This is an illustration from the book of Daniel where the birds came to nest and to find shade in Babylon. Christ applied that same verse to His kingdom. The Gentile nations are "the birds of the air" who have gathered to praise Jesus Christ, the One who in the Old Testament is called "the branch" because He reached out even to us, and we have found rest and shade in His branches.

Leaven

The kingdom of heaven is like leaven (v. 33), the yeast put in meal to sweeten it and make it rise to make bread. A woman would take some leaven and place it in meal which had been crushed and made into flour. This yeast would be placed down in the very center of the flour where it couldn't even be seen. The leaven started growing slowly, but gradually expanded to fill the whole container. That's a picture of the kingdom of God which permeates the believer. When a person trusts in the message of Jesus Christ, the message penetrates so deeply that no one sees external change at first. The transformation starts first in the person's beliefs and gradually spreads to change every aspect of the person's life. The parable of the mustard seed signifies outward growth; the parable of the leaven signifies inward growth. "He who began a good work in you will perfect it unto the day of Christ" (Philippians 1:6).

the treasure and the pearl

Jesus' next two parables were short, but significant: "The kingdom of heaven is like treasure hidden in a field. When a man found it, he hid it again, and then in his joy went and sold all he had and bought that field. Again, the kingdom of heaven is like a merchant looking for fine pearls. When he found one of great value, he went away and sold everything he had and bought it" (vv. 44-46).

In the Old Testament, the nation of Israel is called a treasure (Exodus 19:5), a precious jewel in the hand of God. When Jesus Christ came, Israel was "hidden in the field" — under captivity and ruled by the Gentiles. Yet Jesus saw this treasure. He loved it, wept over it, and purchased it. He gave everything He had, including His life, to redeem a remnant of Israel.

To us, these two parables seem very similar, but Israelites at that time would probably have seen a significance that we don't. The "treasure" might clearly represent Israel, yet Jesus didn't stop there. After the treasure, the merchant found a pearl, and in the nation of Israel, pearls were of little value.

Pearls are formed by oysters in the sea, but Israel was an agricultural people. The high priest's breastplate contained precious stones representing the twelve tribes, none of which was a pearl. Pearls were gathered by the Phoenicians, the Philistines, and the people of the Mediterranean. They weren't found in Israel's Jordan River, Sea of Galilee, or Dead Sea.

In this second parable, the pearl was a symbol of the Gentiles. The merchant first pays the price for the treasure (the elect of Israel), and then pays for the pearl as well (the elect among the Gentiles). Jesus' death paid the price to redeem *everyone*. In John 10:16, Jesus said, "I have other

sheep which are not of this fold. I must bring them also...
They shall be one flock with one shepherd."

At the Feast of Pentecost, which celebrated the gathering
of the harvest, two loaves were symbolically offered to God. It
was a picture of the harvest of Jews and Gentiles. The church
began on the day of Pentecost and continues to this day. In
my congregation, we have a few *treasures*, completed Jews
who have been purchased by God, but the vast majority of
us are *pearls* from Gentile waters, both precious ornaments
to our God.

tHe dRaGnet

After these new concepts of treasure and pearls, Jesus
returns to an older, more familiar one—the image of
judgment as seen in the pulling up of a dragnet (vv. 47-50).
The use of dragnets often is illegal today because nothing
escapes as the net is dragged along the bottom. The dragnet
depicts the final judgment when all men shall be gathered
and judged in the presence of God. This judgment was a
familiar Old Testament concept.

After telling all these parables, Jesus asked his disciples
who had listened attentively, "Have you understood all
these things?" (v. 51) They said, "Yes," and Jesus told them,
"Therefore, every scribe who has become a disciple of the
kingdom is like the head of a household who brings forth out
of his treasure things old and things new" (v. 52).

This was a great way to conclude the section of parables
by Jesus Christ, the master teacher. Scribes were the scholars
of the Old Testament. A "disciple of the kingdom," is a Christian,
a convert to Jesus. (The Apostle Paul was a good example of a
converted scribe.) As these scholars and teachers acquired an
understanding of the kingdom of God, they would be able to
bring out of the treasure of the Word of God things old (truths
from the Old Testament) and things new (instructions for the
church, which would become the New Testament).

Do you see how important these parables are? I don't

think you will understand the life and ministry of Jesus Christ if you don't understand them.

tHe tRainING of tHe tweLve

Chapters 14 to 21 of Matthew are my favorite part of all the gospels: the "withdrawal period" of Jesus Christ. Upon hearing John the Baptist had been decapitated, Jesus withdrew to be alone. Herod had opposed the message of the Christ of God, so he cut off the messenger's head. This was beyond rejection of the Messiah. Blood was now flowing.

After this event until His triumphal entry prior to Easter morning, Jesus did not present Himself to the nation anymore (though people still followed Him around and sought Him out). Instead, He focused on His apostles who would eventually replace the twelve tribes in authority. The emphasis of Matthew 1-13 was the nation, but the emphasis shifts to the twelve in chapters 14-20. Chapter 13 is the pivotal point.

One of the disciples' first lessons is recorded in Matthew 14:13-21. A multitude had come to hear Jesus teach. Jesus had compassion on the multitude, and He healed the sick. As it got later and later in the day, the twelve told Jesus to send the people home to eat because they had come a great distance. But Jesus told his worried disciples, "*You* give them something to eat" (v. 16). This was a first!

How do you train people? You provide them with necessary information, and you give them opportunities to act, but you have to let them succeed or fail. How did you learn to drive? You studied the manual, but you were by no means ready. You had to actually get behind the wheel and put your knowledge into action. Perhaps you made some mistakes and ran over some things you shouldn't have, but that's part of the learning process. You drove with your parents, and they trembled as they helped you through your initial period of trial and error. Finally, when you thought you were ready, you sat beside a gruff-looking officer and took a driver's test.

Eventually, perhaps after several tries, you received a license that said you were a legal driver!

Jesus had been through "the manual" with the twelve (chapters 1-13), and now it was time for them to solo. But they responded the same way we would: "No way!" By this time, they should have known that Jesus had the power to do anything He desired. And He had given them power as well. They should have realized He would never ask anything of *them* that they were incapable of accomplishing. But all they could see was their limited resources.

Andrew said, "We've got a kid here with five loaves of bread and a couple of fish." These loaves were not French loaves. They were small barley rolls and the fish were about the size of hors d'oeuvres. Just imagine the disciples looking at this small bit of food and then looking out at a multitude of more than 5,000 people. One big guy in the front row could put away their entire supply.

So Jesus patiently backed up a step. He changed His instructions from, "You give them something to eat," to, "Bring what you have to Me." Then Jesus did an unusual thing. He took the paltry amount of food the disciples had collected and blessed God for it. Then He broke it and distributed it to the twelve.

I would love to have seen that! "Peter, here's half a roll for you. Here, John, here's your half. Andrew, here's a third half!" And then He started breaking up the puny little fish. Don't you know Doubting Thomas went crazy when he saw what was going on!

Yet the disciples obeyed Him. They went to the multitude, and they gave everything away. I suspect Peter went to the first guy and said, "Here, chew it slow. It's going to have to last, pal!" And when they went back to Jesus empty handed, He gave them some more. They must have asked, "Hey, where'd you get this?" Jesus might have responded, "That's not for you to know. You're just the instrument. Now, go give away what I gave you." What they soon found out, and what we learn as well, is that Jesus' source of supply never runs out—as long as we keep going back. That is the essence of ministry.

After dinner the disciples gathered up twelve baskets of leftovers. Christ's power is more than enough. How many tribes are there in Israel? Twelve. How many baskets to show His sufficiency? Twelve. Christ is sufficient for Israel. Christ fed the multitude this time, but eventually the disciples would have to feed people themselves. When that time came, they would have to pray and trust Him.

I can relate to the way the disciples must have felt during the feeding of the 5,000. In 1973 when I was in college, I had been a Christian only six months when I spoke about my faith to a group of 16 guys at a meeting of the Fellowship of Christian Athletes. Afterward one of the guys in the group said, "Boy, that was great! Would you come speak to the whole school?" I was scared to death, but I agreed! I prayed, "God, if You want me to go, I'll go. I may set the faith back 500 years, but if You want me to, I'm willing to go." I can remember walking out on the Lewisville High School gym floor to the microphone at the free throw line. I peered at 1,500 kids who all looked like members of "The Brady Bunch." I remember my voice cracking and my knees trembling as I told them about God's love, their sin, Christ's death, and salvation by faith. Do you know what happened? The whole crowd silently listened to the gospel—and many responded. I learned, as did the disciples, that God would never fail me.

How much does Jesus want? Everything you have. You go back and forth carrying your pittance to a dying world. And when you finish, you find yourself abounding with leftovers of His goodness because He has blessed you so much. Discipleship is costly. But not following Christ is even more costly. If you don't go, you lose what you have. The only way you get is by giving.

faith in the dark

The next lesson began when Jesus told His disciples to get in the boat and go to the other side (Matthew 14:22).

He didn't go with them, but promised to find them after He stayed and prayed for a while. They left, but as soon as they got on the sea, the winds and waves threatened to sink the boat.

In an earlier instance, Jesus had been with them in the boat, sleeping like Jonah, when a storm struck. The fearful disciples roused Him from His slumber. He spoke to the wind and waves, which instantly became calm, and the disciples saw that He was the Messiah.

This time, however, the disciples are alone in a creaky boat on a stormy sea. Jesus wasn't with them—not physically, anyway. He knew where they were, He knew their problems, and He was praying for them. Eventually He walked out on the water to rescue them.

This miracle represents the next phase of the training of the twelve. Someday they would be sent into the world without Jesus' visible, physical presence. Jesus showed them, in effect, that they could trust Him with their trials even when He wasn't right there with them.

I've been to the Sea of Galilee at night. When the lights go out, it is a black hole. I can't imagine anything scarier than being in that darkness, feeling overwhelmed and hoping that God *really* knows where you are and will take you through. Some of us know the feeling. Jesus has gone away, and we have to trust him in our darkness and our storms. The miracle teaches that He knows where we are. He prays for us, sees us, comes to us, and helps us get where He has told us to go.

I discipled a young man for two years. He lived in my home. Years later, I dedicated his three children in our church. He called recently to tell me the doctors had found a malignant tumor in his wife and they aren't sure she's going to make it. This dear brother can't literally see Christ in this storm, but Christ will take him through this black hole. Some people have gone through divorce, been abandoned by spouses, or buried their children. Some contract a fatal disease or experience some other trauma. When something like this happens to us, we won't see Jesus, but we can be assured that

He will take us through the storm.

true Holiness

Matthew 15 describes how the religious leaders attacked Jesus because He was eating with unwashed hands. He told them it was not what goes into a person's mouth that makes him dirty. Food goes into your belly and out into the latrine and it never touches your heart. Jesus was speaking of the heart, not the belly. In His answer, He established a critical standard for God's people.

God looks for clean people of true piety. This concept of true piety becomes the seminal idea for the book of Galatians: God requires a life of fruitfulness. All the dietary laws were symbols of purity, but with the coming of Christ, they became obsolete. The symbol became real.

the church's future folks

A woman came to Jesus from Tyre and Sidon, a Phoenician area (v. 21). God had made no promises to the Phoenicians, but this woman came to Jesus because her daughter was demon possessed. She said, "Have mercy on me Lord, Son of David." Even as a Phoenician, she invoked the Messiah to act. Jesus didn't answer at first—not because He wasn't compassionate, but it wasn't her time. When the woman fell down to beg Jesus, He responded, "I was sent to the lost sheep of the house of Israel." When the woman persisted, He continued, "It is not good to take bread (Christ) from the children (Israel) and throw it to the dogs (the woman!)." Jesus' statement sounds blunt and cruel, but actually it is very compassionate.

One Greek word for "dogs" refers to nasty mongrels. A different word is used to describe family dogs to whom you would feed leftovers. Before there was Puppy Chow, people fed their pets whatever the kids didn't eat. Jesus used the second word in His comment to the Phoenician woman. His was not an expression of scorn. He was saying something to the effect of, "Lady, I am going to get around to you. You're going to get your bread, but not just yet." The Gentiles would be given to Jesus after His rejection.

But the woman responded with an argument so marvelous that Jesus gave her what she requested. She said, "Yes, Lord, but even the puppies feed on the crumbs that fall from the master's table" (v. 27). She suggested there are some things kids don't want, so they knock them off the table. The dogs get those scraps. They cut in line! The woman was just asking for what Israel didn't want, so Jesus said warmly, "Woman, your faith is great. Be it done to you according to your faith." She understood the power of Jesus and her own need for Him.

After His encounter with one person, Jesus fed a multitude—this time a predominantly Gentile crowd instead of a Jewish one. After this second miraculous feeding, seven baskets of leftovers remained, signifying Christ was not only sufficient for the twelve tribes, but also for the world (seven is the number for completeness). He had no shortage of "crumbs" for the Gentiles. This miracle was prophetic of His ministry to the world.

The Gospel of Matthew is not just a smattering of stories pasted together. It is a cogent argument for the king and the kingdom. And now that Christ is available to the whole world, "There is salvation in no other name other than the One that is named, Jesus Christ." This little mustard seed has branched out to you and me. If you renounce this seed, this offer of life, then you renounce the very Kingdom of God.

There is no plan B.

Reflection/discussion questions

1. Describe people who are represented by each of the four soils. How do they think, act, and respond to Christ? Which are you? Explain.

2. How have you seen the message of the gospel mysteriously leaven...

    ...a person's life?
    ...a church's life?
    ...a community's life?

3. How did Jesus train the twelve? Give examples.

4. Are you involved in this kind of training yourself? If so, how is your life being affected? If not, why not?

5. What would it (or does it) mean for you to live whole-heartedly and unreservedly for Christ?

Chapter 11

new leaders
for a new covenant

The leaders of the Jewish nation, the Pharisees and the Sadducees, had rejected Jesus. They had heard His preaching and seen His miracles, yet they neither repented nor responded. In their unbelief, they asked Him for another sign (Matthew 16:1-4). But Jesus knew they weren't sincere and said the only sign they would see would be the sign of Jonah—a symbol of death and resurrection. With that statement, the die was cast. His death was imminent, irrevocable, and inescapable.

new lessons for new leaders

The religious leaders of Israel did not have the spiritual discernment to understand Jesus, and sometimes neither did those who were closest to Him. Matthew 16:5-12 tells of a time when the disciples had forgotten to take bread with them before crossing a lake. When the topic of bread came up, Jesus said to them, "Beware of the leaven of the Pharisees and Sadducees."

Jesus heard them talking about their worries of everyday life: money, jobs, bills, and payments. He interrupted them with a play on words. Jesus wasn't concerned about the physical bread they didn't have. Instead, He was concerned about the spiritual "leaven" that they might have. "The leaven of the Pharisees" was hypocrisy. The leaven of the Sadducees was unbelief. In the Bible, "leaven" is often a picture of sin. It's something that Israel brought from Egypt. It starts small, but it spreads quickly if unchecked.

Sin affects people the same way leaven affects bread dough. Proverbs says, "Guard your heart, my son, for out of it comes the issues of life" (Proverbs 4:23). The message is: Watch your heart so evil won't take over. You can't compartmentalize sin in your life. It's leaven. It'll spread. It'll get you.

a change of priorities

The disciples, however, weren't thinking of spiritual truth. They were bemoaning the fact they didn't have physical bread for their physical bodies. Jesus told them not to worry about their physical needs: "You men of little faith. Why do you discuss among yourselves that you have no bread? Don't you understand yet or remember the five loaves of the 5,000? How many baskets did you take up? (The answer is 12, fellows.) Of the seven loaves of the 4,000, how many large baskets did you take up? (The answer is seven, guys. Remember?) Therefore, how is it that you don't understand? I did not speak to you concerning bread." Jesus meant, "I can take care of you. I can give you all the bread you can handle. Don't be so concerned about your physical, surface, tangible needs. I take care of the birds and the flowers. Shall I not much more take care of you?" He reminded them to seek first

His kingdom and His righteousness. His message to them was, "I want you to shift your priorities."

Christians should realize that life is more than jobs, food, money, and fuel for our bodies to do the next day's work. We live for a future day. We have a higher enlightenment than other people. Our first priority should be to fulfill our spiritual needs rather than our physical ones. "Seek first the kingdom and its righteousness, and all these things shall be added unto you."

You have probably seen this to be true. More than likely you know people who are desperately passionate about the things of this world, yet whose lives are miserable because sin prevents them from walking with God. On the other hand, you may also know people who allow God to take care of them. They enjoy each day's provision. They may earn a lot of money—or very little—but their priority is their relationship with God. When those people die, their funerals are packed with people whose lives were deeply touched by them.

a philippian reminder

Paul provides a good reminder of these facts in Philippians 4. He starts by reminding us to, "Rejoice in the Lord always. Again, I'll say rejoice!" (v. 4) He's our joy. And the things of this world? Paul says, "Let your moderation be known to all men. The Lord is near" (v. 5). Christ is coming. Don't invest in perishable things. Don't be straightening pictures in burning buildings or swabbing the deck of the Titanic! It's going down! Let your moderation in things of the earth be obvious to all men because Christ is coming soon. Paul continued, "Be anxious in nothing, but by prayer and supplication and thanksgiving, let your requests be made known to God. And the peace of God [because your priorities are right], which passes all understanding, will guard your hearts and minds in Christ Jesus" (vv. 6-7). This means: Put the things of the world on the back burner.

Paul concluded, "Finally brethren, the things that are true, honorable, right, pure, lovely, of good repute, praiseworthy, and excellent, let your minds dwell on these things" (v. 8). Peter said it like this: "Fix your hope completely on the glory to be revealed to you at the coming of Jesus Christ. Gird up your loins for action." Don't stumble because you are entangled in the things of the earth. Put your hope completely in His coming. This is the same message Jesus gave to the twelve.

As Christians, we have inside information about where this world is going. Travel light while you're here. Don't get entangled. Don't be worried. Some of us don't spend time in prayer and the Word, and we haven't learned how to share our faith. Those things don't matter much to us because we are desperately concerned about tomorrow's workday, Friday's paycheck, and our credit card debt. But to prevent our worries from incapacitating us, we must pay attention to what Jesus is telling His disciples. He prepared them for a new place of leadership in a new program. They were to become a heavenly-minded band.

installation of new Leadership

A key to understanding the entire life of Christ is contained in Matthew chapters 16 and 17. When Jesus came into the region of Caesarea Philippi, he asked his disciples, "Who do men say that I, the Son of Man, am?" (Matthew 16:13) Opinions of the crowds were varied: John the Baptist, Elijah, Jeremiah, or one of the prophets. In other words, many people then saw Jesus as a great man, even a supernatural man—but not God. And that's the way many people still see Christ. They deeply respect Him, they learn from Him, and they admire Him, but they are not about to concede that He is God.

Then Jesus got more personal with His disciples: "But what about you? Who do you say I am?" (v. 15) Peter's answer differed from the crowd's: "Thou art the Christ, the Son of the living God." Jesus responded, "Blessed are you Simon Barjonah; for flesh and blood hath not revealed it unto thee, but my Father which is in heaven."

Jesus said Peter was blessed because his knowledge of Christ was not the result of "flesh and blood" (human intuition, wisdom, knowledge, and righteousness). Peter's revelation came from God. Paul told the Corinthians, "No one can say Jesus is Lord save through the Holy Spirit" (I Corinthians 12:3). Saving faith is not something that can be acquired through human energy. Heaven does not contain people who are smarter than others. Believers are people who have been called. God revealed Christ to them because God predetermined where they would spend eternity. He loved them from the foundation of the world. God's sovereign mercies enabled us to know Christ. Heaven revealed Him to us. Paul said to the Corinthians, "Things which eye has not seen, things which ear hath not heard, which have not entered into the heart of man, God has prepared for those that love him" (I Corinthians 2:9). We don't become Christians because we think our way through it.

Jesus continued, "And I say also unto thee, thou art Peter, and upon this rock I will build my church, and the gates of hell shall not prevail against it" (Matthew 16:18). Jesus changed Peter's name, just as He did Abraham and Sarah's. But he also used "*this* rock," not "*you*." "The rock" was something else besides Peter.

What is the rock the church is built on? Is it Peter? I hope not! Peter denied Christ. He was later rebuked by Paul for compromise (Galatians 2). If not Peter, who is this rock? The Bible says, "The stone that the builders rejected, this has become the cornerstone" (I Peter 2:7). "Christ is the cornerstone" (Ephesians 2:20). Jesus is The Rock, and the church is built upon Him. Notice that men do not build, Christ does. He ordains, He calls, He converts, He sanctifies, and He will raise from the dead. "No man can lay a foundation other than... Christ" (I Corinthians 3:11).

Jesus offered Himself first to the nation Israel as their prophet and their king, but they rejected Him. At this point He is preparing to go to the cross where He will die as our priest and our mediator. He is turning from Israel to the church. This is a new world order.

the men in charge

When Christ is gone, who is going to be in authority? There will be some new "rocks" on this foundation. Speaking to Peter, Jesus says, "I will give you the keys of the kingdom." When you give keys to someone, entrust that person to be a steward. You give him responsibility in your house. In the Old Testament, stewards were given keys to the house and had complete authority to carry out the master's will, particularly in the care and feeding of His children. If the master said "No," the steward didn't do it. If the master said "Yes," then it was unquestioned. He "bound and loosed" according to the Master's pleasure.

Peter is installed as the leader of the twelve. All the leaders of Israel are fired from their jobs. They failed as spiritual leaders and are not going to lead the church! As the leader and spokesman of the twelve, Peter now has the keys as the apostles become the stewards of Jesus' authority.

Jesus said, "Whatsoever thou shalt bind on earth shall be bound in heaven; and whatsoever thou shalt loose on earth shall be loosed in heaven" (Matthew 16:19). Jesus didn't explain what He was talking about to the twelve because they readily understood. His reference is a paraphrase of an Old Testament story found in Isaiah 22. A worthless scribe named Shebna was a steward of the house of David, but God fired him. Isaiah said, "Shebna, what do you have for yourself here that you have hewn out a tomb for your greatness? Behold, God shall take you like a ball and wad you up and cast you in a distant country." And God did just that. Then Isaiah turned to Eliakim, who was a godly man, and gave him the keys to the house of David. And God said, "And whatever you bind will be bound and whatever you loose shall be loosed." The disciples understood this story.

As the curtain fell on Israel, Jesus instructed them to tell no one He was Messiah. Then He unveiled the hard, cold truth about His imminent execution (v. 21). This was the first explicit mention of the death of Jesus. "From that time, Jesus Christ began to show his disciples that He must go to Jerusalem, suffer many things from the elders, chief priests and scribes, be killed and raised on the third day." As you read His comments, you may not have any problem understanding what He meant. We look back at those events with the perspective of New Testament theology. But if you had been one of the twelve and your Scriptures taught that Messiah would come and reign over the earth with Israel as His glory, what would you say? You might say what Peter said, "God forbid it!" (v. 22) Peter tried to keep Christ off the cross simply because he didn't yet have the benefit of complete New Testament revelation. He didn't yet realize that he couldn't have a kingdom without a cross.

Peter expected the Messiah to rule. But Jesus said, in essence, "Not only am I going to die, Peter, but you're going to die, too. I'm going to a cross, and anyone who follows Me will have to bear his cross, too" (vv. 23-26). People who follow Christ must be willing to follow Him publicly, to be persecuted, and even to lose their friends or their lives. How do you know a person's faith is real? Watch and see how he or she goes through suffering. The one who endures and grows in his faith has the real thing!

But after presenting His expectations for His followers, Jesus offered some encouragement (vv. 26-28). The disciples began to realize the coming of Christ's kingdom wasn't everything they had expected: blessedness, glory, destruction of their enemies, and a king with a royal, purple robe. They had misunderstood, but His kingdom was still real and was awaiting them. The plan of God involves pain and death—and then glory.

Jesus confirmed God's ultimate justice: "The Son of Man will come in the glory of his Father with his angels, and He will pay back every man for what he has done according to his deeds. Truly I say to you, some of you standing here will not taste death until you see the kingdom" (vv. 27-28). If the disciples still had questions, it didn't take them long to figure out what Jesus meant by this last statement. Soon He would confirm their hopes with a glorious vision of His deity.

assurance on the mountain

The next scene Matthew describes (as well as Mark and Luke) is the transfiguration of Jesus (Matthew 17:1-13). Jesus took Peter, James, and John up on a mountain where they witnessed Him transfigured in glory. Elijah and Moses appeared as well. Moses (the law) and Elijah (the prophets) embodied the entire Old Testament. All of a sudden, the glory descended upon them as if they were in the Holy of Holies! Peter, James, and John trembled, and they heard God speak! God said, "This is my beloved Son, in whom I am well-pleased. Listen to Him" (Matthew 17:5). God reminded them of His promise in Deuteronomy 18:15 to raise up a prophet like Moses to mediate for them. "When He comes, you shall listen to Him." The voice of God means, "*This* is the final mediator! Pay attention!"

I've read many books and articles which address the purpose of the transfiguration. Some say Jesus was sad and needed to be encouraged, but that's way off base. The purpose of the transfiguration was that our Lord had just rejected the leaders of Israel and appointed the twelve to spread the word about His new plan. He had explained to them how the church was going to be built upon His death and resurrection, but they didn't understand it. Jesus encouraged them by assuring them He was going to come back. To prove it, He took them up on a mountain where they saw their King, the fulfillment of the Old Testament, the One the Father approved. The purpose of the transfiguration is clearly explained in II Peter 1:16: "We did not follow cleverly devised tales when we made known to you the coming of our Lord Jesus." That means that when the writers of Scripture were talking of Jesus' coming to rule of the world, they weren't making it up. Peter said, "We were eyewitnesses of His majesty."

The transfiguration was a picture of the future, a taste of glory, an encouragement to believe. The Messiah would die, and the disciples would die, also—many in violent ways. But their faith was strengthened from this glimpse of Jesus in His glory during His transfiguration. In II Peter 1:19, Peter summed up the impact of the transfiguration, "...and so we have the prophetic word made more certain."

If you have taken up your cross and followed Christ, you may have lost your friends, but you have stood fast on the gospel. You have been hated by those who love the world. Eventually, you may even die for your faith. When the day comes when your heart beats for the last time and your breath leaves your body, those at your bed side will wonder why you have a smile on your face. You can be sure you will be in God's kingdom because all your hopes are in One who will not lose. You also have the prophetic word of His kingdom "made certain" through the transfiguration.

There is a tale of a king who was close to death, and wondered who would take over his empire. He said to his three sons, "I want you to climb the mountain ridge. The one who climbs highest is the one who will lead in my place." The first son came back late in the afternoon, holding a twig. He said, "Father, this is from the last tree where the trees stop growing. I've climbed up beyond them." The next son came back with a feather and said, "Father, I've climbed beyond where the trees stop, to where the rocks lie. I've gone to the very eagle's nest. And there on the highest crag, I've taken a feather from an eagle." Just as night was beginning to fall, in came the third son. He had nothing in his hands. He said, "Father, I've gone beyond where the great trees grow and where the great rocks lie, and I've gone beyond the eagle's nest. I have gone to the very top. I bring you nothing in my hand, but I have a vision of what is on the other side."

That's the significance of the transfiguration. If we know categorically that this earth shall be no more, but that the Messiah will come and recompense every man according to his deeds, we can take up our crosses and die willingly. We've seen a vision of the other side.

Reflection/discussion questions

1.   What are the goals and purposes of most of the people you know? What are some of the results?

2.   What does it mean to "travel light here on earth"?

3.   What does the transfiguration's implied promise mean to you?

4.   In what ways are you living for eternity? What is the cost/benefit ratio?

5.   In what ways are you living for today? What is the cost/benefit ratio?

Chapter 12

people who make a difference

Immediately after Jesus' transfiguration, a particular miracle occurs. Matthew 17:14 introduces the characters involved. "And when they [Jesus, Peter, James, and John] came to the multitude, a man came up to him [Jesus], falling on his knees before him and saying, 'Lord, have mercy on my son. He is a lunatic.'"

The word *lunatic* literally means "moon struck." This boy had evidences of demon possession. He suffered a violent form of seizures which threw him into the fire and into water on occasion. The condition had existed from his youth. In those days, people believed this problem was caused by the moon, so he is called "a moonstruck person," a child of the darkness. Interestingly, Mark's Gospel records the father's words as, "This is my son, my only son." Do you remember hearing something similar to this statement connected to the transfiguration? On the mountain God the Father had said, "This is My Son whom I love." Jesus came down the mountain and found another father showing concern for his beloved son. The Father on the mountain was full of joy, but the father in the valley was full of pain and despair. One is the Son of light; the other is a son of darkness. One is a Son controlled by God; the other is thrashed by demons. In the valley, the two sons meet.

The father told Jesus, "I brought him to your disciples, and they could not cure him" (v. 16). Jesus answered, "Unbelieving and perverted generation, how long shall I be with you?" (v. 17). That rebuke was addressed to the Pharisees, not the disciples. The Jewish leaders of the day were using this tragic, demonic boy to test Jesus and see if He would perform a miracle. The disciples were unable to cast out the evil spirit. But Jesus exercised His power and rebuked the demon, and it came out of the boy at once.

Later, the disciples came to Jesus privately and wanted to know why they couldn't cast it out (v. 19). Jesus told them their failure was due to the smallness of their faith. Earlier Jesus had sent them out with the ability to cast out demons (Matthew 10:1). Here, they followed that plan and said the right words, but they had no faith and no prayer. A Christian leader can never trust in yesterday's system. Prayer is required on a regular basis. And another requirement, according to Jesus, is faith the size of a mustard seed (Matthew 17:20-21). Great mountains can be moved by little acts of faith which are empowered through prayer. This miracle is recorded in three gospels, and it always follows the account of the transfiguration. It communicates an essential lesson for believers of all times.

faith in the valley

Why is this miracle connected with the account of the transfiguration? The faith that had been affirmed by witnessing the glorious transfiguration must be put into action at the foot of the mountain where people actually live. We are awed by the eye-opening "mountaintop" experiences of faith, but those are rare and special times. We cannot (and should not) live on mountaintops. We must descend into the valley of our dark world.

Jesus Christ revealed His glory to a chosen few in a remote place, but they had to come down that mountain to the valley. Beloved sons lived there—not beloved sons of God, but beloved children of darkness. In the valley, people felt enormous pain and despair. Rather than praying, expecting, and witnessing wonderful things, the disciples now entered into dialogue with unbelieving religious leaders. But dialogue is all talk and no power. Jesus showed His infinite grace and power and explained, "The reason you didn't work a miracle is because you didn't trust and you didn't pray."

Tony Evans, one of the greatest expositors in the church and pastor of Oak Cliff Fellowship in Dallas, tells a joke to illustrate this text. A man (who just happened to be from an anonymous Texas Agricultural and Mechanical University) bought a chain saw. But the next day he returned the chain saw and complained to the store manager, "This sorry thing won't work! I cut down one tree, but that was all I could do. It wore me out! It was cumbersome and heavy. I was doing a whole lot better with a regular handsaw." So the store manager inspected it. As soon as he started it up and the chain saw roared, the guy exclaimed, "What's that sound?" Tony Evans used this story as a picture of the church. The guy possessed something that should have been useful and valuable, but was worthless unless he employed its power. That's the image of too many people in the church.

Christians love to congregate. We love to construct elaborate buildings and admire their glory, but Jesus will not let us stay there. We cannot shut ourselves away from the rest of the world to worship the only begotten Son on a spiritual mountaintop—not permanently, anyway. There are hurting children in the valley whose fathers are weeping. Children are being destroyed. The devil has them in his grip. We need to go to them, and when we encounter them we will need faith and power. We must pray and trust God.

When I was at Dallas Theological Seminary, my emphasis was in church history. Among the finest church historians I've ever heard is Dr. John Hannah, who taught us that all revivals are preceded by Christians who become convicted of three things:

1.   the greatness of their commission;
2.   the littleness of their abilities;
3.   the power of God.

When we confront the horrors of the world around us in light of these three things, we are driven to seek mercy that can only come from God. Then great things happen. But Dr. Hannah noted that prayer does not precede great revivals. He said, "Prayer *is* the revival, because it is far easier for God to convert a heathen than it is to make His children pray." We don't pray because we are too busy to hear the cries of dying people. When we *do* hear, we tend to turn to God, and revival is the result.

Do you pray? Are you praying regularly for people who have broken your heart, whom you long for God to bring to faith because you know you can't do it? In his writings, Paul frequently asked people to pray for him. Why? Because he knew the greatness of his commission, the littleness of his own abilities, and the might of God. His heart was broken for a world filled with sheep without a shepherd.

If you want to see how much fun the Christian life can be, get together with a bunch of people who commit themselves to keep praying until they see God do marvelous things. Usually, He doesn't change the problem until He first changes the person. You can't stay on the mountain. But when you go down in the valley where the people are, you discover God is there as well.

the necessity of integrity

From Jesus' dramatic casting out of a demon, we move to what is perhaps the most obscure miracle in the New Testament. It started with an accusatory question that had little to do with spiritual things. Tax collectors approached Peter and asked, "Does not your teacher pay the two drachma tax?" (Matthew 17:24)

This half-shekel tax had been instituted in the book of Exodus for the upkeep of the tabernacle. The tax was not imperative in Jesus' day; it was optional because the original temple had been destroyed. It might be that Jewish religious leaders prodded the tax collectors to ask this question because they wanted to catch Jesus doing something wrong. Some people still enjoy looking for small areas of inconsistency in a Christian's life, and perhaps you can identify with Jesus or Peter in this situation. Peter responded to the tax collector, "Yes, we'll pay." He knew Jesus would be obedient.

Jesus used this circumstance to teach Peter a lesson. He asked him, "What do you think, Simon? From whom do the kings of the earth collect customs: from their sons or strangers?" (v. 25) At this time, when Rome conquered a province, they collected a tax. But the tax wasn't paid by native Romans; it came from the conquered people. Since the tax was collected "from strangers," Jesus knew that "the sons are exempt" (v. 26).

The temple was God's residence, and Jesus was God's Son. He was a native citizen of heaven, and as such, certainly was not expected to pay a tax for the upkeep of His own temple. But Peter's lesson continued with Jesus' next words, "But lest we give them offense..." (v. 27). Jesus knew He had the legitimate right to refuse to pay this particular tax. But He also knew this was not really such a big deal, so He told Peter, "Go to the sea, throw in a hook, and take the first fish that comes up." Peter obeyed, and the fish's mouth contained not only the tax for Jesus, but enough for Peter, too. Here is yet another lesson from Jesus for Peter: "Not only am I a Son of the King, but Peter, you are, too!"

What's the purpose of recording this event? This little miracle shows that God is concerned about our reputations in seemingly small choices which can bring honor or disgrace. Legally, Jesus didn't have to pay this tax. But He wanted to glorify God and protect His reputation. A believer chooses to limit his freedom because God's reputation is more important than any individual's freedoms.

BEING faithful in the little things

These two miracles, one dramatic and public, the other private and obscure, provide a helpful contrast for Christians today. First, we ought to pray that God will do great things in using us to deliver wicked men from their evil. But when we get in our cars after the prayer meeting, we ought to drive the speed limit. Living for God means that little things count: stopping at stop signs, being completely honest on your income tax, and voluntarily limiting your legitimate freedoms to avoid conflict with someone who might be offended by such behavior. These two miracles are recorded side by side because God is honored just as much by the little things we do for Him as He is in our great proclamations about Him.

Some time ago, I went skiing with a friend from Vancouver, Canada. I noticed he was wearing a small steel pinky ring. I asked about it and he told me people get these rings when they graduate from engineering school in Vancouver. He explained that in the early 1900s, engineers built the Second Narrows Bridge in Vancouver. They thought the design was perfect, but they miscalculated the size of the bolts needed for the span on the bridge. The designed bolts were too small to support the weight they carried. As a result, the bolts sheared off and the bridge collapsed, taking the lives of 11 men. The engineering school collected and kept those sheared bolts. Now, when a person graduates, a bolt is taken out of storage, melted down, and formed into a ring. All engineering graduates wear the ring on the smallest finger of their right hands. My friend said, "As we work on our drawings, that ring clicks on the pencil or drawing board. As we draw, our eyes fall on that ring. It reminds us that one small act of negligence can result in disaster."

That's the message of this text. Little acts of spiritual negligence or moral disobedience can bring disaster to the body of Christ. God's reputation is more important than our freedom.

What are some of these little acts of disobedience? When some people get angry, they allow a "hell" or a "damn" to slip out. Those are little words and seemingly insignificant in light of about 50,000 worse things. But a testimony about Christ may be discredited by a lost person if that person is put off by swearing. Other "little" things we need to watch out for include gossip, seductive clothing styles, questionable humor, and our choice of music, television programs, and movies. Keeping your reputation clean and blameless is important to God.

As the saying goes: For lack of a nail, there perished a shoe. For lack of a shoe, there perished a horse. For lack of a horse, there perished a rider. For lack of a rider, there perished a soldier, which turned the tide of a battle, which determined a war. All for the lack of a nail. Little things can make a big difference.

kids' stuff

Effective leadership also requires attention to "little people." During the time of Jesus, spiritual leadership had taken a complete departure from the Old Testament model. Spirituality had become associated with power, wealth, status, and clout. If you were poor, small, debilitated, handicapped, or female, you were looked down upon because you lacked status and power. Yet these were the people to whom Jesus ministered. He even spent a lot of time with Jewish tax collectors who had sold out their fellow Israelites to get good Roman jobs. Jesus' behavior confused the disciples. So they asked Him flat out, "Who is the greatest in the kingdom?"

In response, Jesus selected a small child to stand in the center of their circle and said, "Unless you become like a little child, you cannot enter the kingdom" (Matthew 18:1-3). A child has no wisdom of his own to draw from. He trusts his father to protect, to provide, and to guide. That's what it takes to become a Christian. In spite of all your degrees, power, and wealth, you have to become like a child and learn to rely completely on someone else. It's humbling to admit our neediness and ignorance. But all the worldly wisdom you can acquire will not be enough to allow you to know God. Again we see a focus on little things. The way to God is by faith like a little child. We are all "little people" to God.

Jesus then gave a stern warning to leaders who misuse their position and cause His children to stumble (vv. 6-10). Leaders should be gentle servants. They shouldn't dominate their flocks. Sometimes a leader has to make hard decisions, but he is still a servant because he reports to God. Sometimes we hear horror stories of people in the ministry accused of child abuse, adultery, fraud, and stealing. Jesus' words are a warning to spiritual leaders to be careful how they treat the little people entrusted to their care.

Jesus also gave His disciples some insight on how God views little children. Christian leaders should be kind toward God's children because "their angels behold the face of my Father which is in heaven" (v. 10). I agree with rabbinic literature that taught there were levels in the angelic realm. Certain angels have the privilege of beholding the very face of God, and those angels are watching over the weakest of the saints. When Christians crawl into the lap of the Savior because they realize they can do nothing else to enter the kingdom, it is critical that we love and honor them. The angels in the presence of God look after them.

When given the opportunity to minister to the family of God, use your position to help others out rather than using people to help you "climb the ladder." Leaders are called to be servants. This may be a dramatic shift in thinking from some of the modern management techniques. But it's the only way that works.

Reflection/discussion questions

1. What are some evidences of God's power at work in a person's life?

2. Reflect on Dr. Hannah's statement about revivals. Do you hear the cries of dying people, or are you too busy to hear them? Explain.

3. What would encourage you to pray more?

4. What are some "little things" which color a person's integrity and reputation in our culture? How are you doing in each of those areas?

5. What does it mean to "come to Christ as a little child"? Is that image attractive or offensive to you? Why?

Chapter 13

unity, HOLY matrimony, and tHe secret of gREatness

Once a man in our congregation brought a business associate to visit our church. As soon as his guest walked in the door, he saw a man who had cheated him in a business deal. The guest stopped, turned in his tracks, and walked back out. If you asked him what he thought of Denton Bible Church, he would tell you that we are an unworthy congregation of people. There were 2,600 people in attendance that day, and 2,599 of us were indicted because of the actions of one person.

As we pick up where we left off in Matthew 18, Jesus teaches that we are to be people who are unified in holiness. Sin is a rampant reality, so what do you do when one Christian begins to take advantage or even injure another? As much as we might like to deny it, people in Christian churches cheat on their spouses, engage in abuse, swindle their clients, gossip, and commit all sorts of atrocious acts. Does a commitment to unity mean you do away with moral standards and turn a blind eye to avoid conflict? Jesus instructs these new leaders in a program of conflict management.

conflict management

When Jesus said, "If your brother sins..." (v. 15), sin is not the everyday sin we all deal with. This type of sin is specific, and is later mentioned in Galatians 6:1 in regard to being "caught in a trespass." It refers to an intentional, verifiable offense that harms another person. How should we respond to such sins?

The first step should always be to have the courage to go to the offender in private and try to resolve the problem. "If he repents, you have won your brother" (v. 15). Paul instructed the Galatians to "restore such a one in a spirit of gentleness." Our role is not to punish. Don't respond in wrath or revenge. Try to restore the person gently. Don't try to harm him.

But if the person who has sinned is resistant, don't resort to gossip. Take two or more witnesses (people who actually saw the offense, not just people who are on your side) and go back to the person. Sit down and talk it through again. Let the witnesses speak, not to harm the person, but to restore him. The motive should still be love —not punishment.

If the person still refuses to respond, tell an elder of the church who brings the matter before the membership. At this point, the person has been given three chances to repent.

If the person still refuses to respond to the church or its leadership, according to Jesus he "becomes to you as a Gentile or a tax gatherer" (v. 17.) Within the Jewish community, a tax gatherer was regarded as an unbeliever. A Gentile was an alien in Israel, obviously not received into the fellowship of the nation. People within the church who refuse to repent of their offenses, even after the issue has become a matter of church business, are to be treated as unbelievers. In our church, that means the person can attend church services but cannot take communion, have any official position in the church, join a discipleship group, or teach Sunday School. He is regarded as an unbeliever because he has a "thrice-hardened" attitude toward the Word of God.

Yes, the goal of our body is unity, but it is a rugged, vigorous unity. We are not a flaccid, ambivalent, ambiguous group of people! Our unity is based on righteousness and truth.

Someone might wonder, "Aren't you harsh to dictate what is right and wrong?" Jesus answers, "Truly I say to you, whatever you bind on earth shall be bound in heaven" (v. 18). The church has been given a divine standard of morality. That which we bind has already been bound by God. We simply reflect a heavenly morality because the church is to be the kingdom of God. If heaven doesn't have adultery, swindlers, or gossip, then neither should the church. Everyone else in the city might slander, hate, fornicate and do anything they want. They aren't Christians; they aren't in the kingdom of God. But we are the church, and must abide by God's standard. The unity of the church body is tremendously important because it determines the power of our prayers. According to Jesus, "If two of you agree on earth about anything that they may ask, it shall be done for them by my Father who is in heaven. For where two or three have gathered in my name, there is my presence" (vv. 19-20).

A church that does not enforce doctrine, truth, and holiness forfeits God's active presence. A man who wasn't a Christian once said, "There are more rules for riding a bus than for joining a Christian church." His statement is sad, but true. On a bus you can't smoke, you can't stand up, and you can't be rowdy. Yet in many churches, you can do almost anything you want to, and nobody will say anything for the sake of "Christian unity." But Jesus makes it clear that His presence is not in such places. The process of reproof, repentance, and restoration keeps the church pure and insures that God's presence is there in full strength.

At Denton Bible Church, we've reached stage four (treating unrepentant people as unbelievers) only a few times. The process is not meant to reach stage four. Problems and offenses are meant to be resolved privately or with only a few involved. But we've had a few cases where people simply would not repent in the areas of immorality and fraudulent business practices.

foRGiven and foRGiVinG

Perhaps people would be quicker to repent if they knew others would be quicker to forgive. Rheumatoid arthritis occurs when a person's immune system gets confused and begins to attack the joints. It is painful indeed! Sometimes the "immune system" of the church (truth and righteousness) takes a judgmental turn and members begin to attack one another. Without the lubricating fluid of forgiveness, the body of Christ becomes stiff, hard, unforgiving, caustic, censorious, and unloving. This is crippling to the body of Christ.

Peter heard Jesus talk about forgiveness, and he asked, "How often do I have to forgive my brother? Up to seven times?" (Matthew 18:21) The rabbis of that day taught people to forgive offenders three times. Peter doubled that number and added one for good measure. That must have seemed pretty good to him! But Jesus responded, "No, you forgive him seventy times seven." In other words, forgive people as infinitely as God has forgiven you. Unity is maintained by humility (vv. 1-14), truth (vv. 15-20), and forgiveness (vv. 21-35).

To illustrate this point, Jesus told a story: "The kingdom of heaven may be compared to a certain king who wished to settle accounts with his slaves. And when he had begun to settle them, there was brought to him one who owed him 10,000 talents. And since he did not have the means to repay, the lord commanded him to be sold, along with his wife and children and all that he had, and repayment to be made. And the slave prostrated himself and said, 'Have patience with me, and I will repay you everything!'" (vv. 23-26). By today's standards, this guy owed $18 million! His promise to repay the debt is humorous indeed! How do you repay $18 million—in nine $2 million installments? This guy is not only foolish and in debt; he's delirious about his ability to handle the situation!

Jesus continued His lesson, "The lord of that slave felt moved and he forgave him everything" (v. 27). The master hurt for that man. He felt compassion for him. What a lowly servant! What a matchless master! Who is the magnificent lord who forgives all? It's God. Who's the lowly slave who has a debt he cannot pay? That's you and me. We owed God an infinite debt, and there was nothing we could do to pay it off.

But Jesus' story isn't over yet. The forgiven slave went out and found a fellow slave who owed him 100 denarii—about a third of a year's wage. The slave grabbed this fellow servant by the neck and choked him and said, "Pay back what you owe!" Even his fellow slaves were offended by his behavior. The second slave fell down and began to beg with the very words the first one had used, "Have patience and I will repay you." But the slave who had been released from an $18 million debt was unwilling to forgive a debt that was miniscule in comparison, and he threw his debtor into prison. When other slaves saw what happened, they were deeply grieved and told their lord what had happened. Summoning the first slave, the lord said, "You wicked slave. I forgave you all that debt because you entreated me. Should you not also have had mercy on your fellow slave, even as I had mercy on you?" (vv. 32-33)

God forgives us on the basis of Christ's death, which paid the price for our sin, yet you and I forgive on the basis of our own depravity. Did you catch that? God forgives because He is just. We free others and forgive them because of our own inexplicable wickedness. How can I refuse to forgive a small offense against me when God has forgiven me for an offense I could *never* repay? Unforgiveness is the quality of a reprobate non-Christian. But because of the mercy I have received, I am expected to grant mercy. A woman once said to John Wesley, "I do not forgive." Wesley replied, "I trust you do not sin."

As Jesus concluded His story, we see that the slave who demanded justice over mercy was shown what justice without mercy felt like. "And the lord moved with anger, handed him over to the torturers until he should repay all that was owed him. So shall my heavenly Father do also to you if each of you does not forgive his brother from his heart" (vv. 34-35).

Don't be alarmed by this text. It's not about losing your salvation. The New Testament is clear. Forgiven people do not habitually harbor unforgiveness. Unforgiveness is the quality of someone who is self-righteous, not someone overwhelmed with God's gracious mercy.

What do you do about a person who has offended you? You don't have to like the person. You don't have to rehire him or let her babysit. You don't have to send her a Christmas card. If someone has hurt me and his name comes up in a conversation, his face crosses my field of vision like a metal duck at a carnival. And I want to shoot him! But I refuse to slander him. Instead, I pray. Jesus told His disciples, "Pray for those that abuse you, greet those that have harmed you." In public, treat them with kindness. In other words, treat them as God has treated you.

Praying for people on your "hit list" is a painful thing to do. I know that for a fact. And I am comforted by Jesus' teaching on this subject. In Luke 17 is what I think is the most comforting parable in the New Testament about forgiveness. Jesus said, "Be on your guard. If your brother sins, rebuke him. If he repents, forgive him" (Luke 17:3). So far, so good. We have to be on our guard because we have a tendency to be unforgiving. But Jesus continues, "If he sins against you seven times a day and returns seven times saying, 'I repent,' then forgive him" (v. 4). In other words, my forgiveness is not to be based on how I feel. If someone hurts me seven times in a single day and returns each time to apologize, I may have doubts about the person's sincerity! But still, I'm not supposed to exact judgment against him. My view of his character may decline, but I'm still not to slander him. I'm to forgive him every time.

When the apostles heard this, they said, "Lord, increase our faith" (Luke 17:5). They realized great faith would be required in order to respond in such a manner, but Jesus told them they didn't need great faith, only "mustard seed" faith of simple obedience.

Jesus said, "Which of you, when you have a slave plowing or tending sheep, will say to him when he is come in from the field, 'Come immediately, sit down and eat.' Will he not say to him, 'Prepare something for me to eat, properly clothe yourself, serve me until I have eaten and drunk and afterward you will eat and drink'? He does not thank the slave because he did all the things that were commanded of him, does he?"

In other words, a slave works all day plowing the field. When he comes in, he is famished. He wants a hot bath followed by a big plate of roast beef, corn on the cob with butter running down the sides, mashed potatoes with gravy, and a big glass of sweetened iced tea. But the slave works for his master, and he does what he is supposed to do. Feeding the master takes priority over feeding himself.

Employers expect as much from their employees, don't they? At 8 o'clock Monday morning, many of us might prefer to sleep late. Yet our bosses expect us to punch in, and they don't care if we don't feel like working that day. Even when we work hard at our jobs, our bosses don't always thank us because we're just doing what we are supposed to do.

Jesus says we should consider it our duty to do the things that have been commanded of us. Remember that the context here is forgiveness. So when we are offended by someone, we should forgive because that's what we've been instructed to do. It doesn't matter whether or not we feel like it or particularly want to be forgiving.

When you think about forgiving certain people, your spirit probably rebels against the thought just as mine does. I don't like to forgive people who hurt me. I feel like slandering them, but I choose to forgive because God told me to. In one sense, there's nothing spiritual about this parable in Luke 17. Forgiveness is an act of obedience apart from feelings or in spite of them. In another sense, this parable is very comforting because it teaches that I don't have to feel forgiving in order to forgive someone. I simply obey.

marriage: meant to last

Moving back to the book of Matthew, we find another hot, current topic for the church. During the time Jesus was teaching, marriages were in a horrendous state. As a matter of fact, men could divorce their wives for almost any reason. So the topic came up in one of the encounters between Jesus and the religious leaders. Their question came from the Old Testament: "Is it lawful for a man to divorce his wife for any cause at all?" (Matthew 19:3)

Their question was a reference to Deuteronomy 24:1: "When a man takes a wife and marries her and it happens that she finds no favor in his eyes because he has found some indecency in her, he writes her a certificate of divorce and puts it in her hand and sends her out."

Obviously God did not endorse divorce at creation when He said, "A man shall leave his father and mother and cleave to his wife, and the two shall become one flesh" (Genesis 2:24). What God joins, men don't separate. But God knew the hardness of the human heart. So God reluctantly allowed divorce under certain specific circumstances. To the best of my knowledge, a woman could not divorce her husband, but a man could divorce his wife. God's strict rules were given to discourage divorce. The Deuteronomy passage required an official decree so that divorce couldn't be an impulsive act. The decision was final. If a man divorced his wife and she remarried and her second husband also sent her away, she could not return to her first husband. New Testament teaching calls for reconciliation in cases of marital separation. Paul wrote that if someone left a mate, the person was to be reconciled to the mate or else remain unmarried (I Corinthians 7:10-11).

Key to the argument about what was or wasn't acceptable was the interpretation of *indecency*, found in the Deuteronomy 24 passage. There were two schools of thought in Israel. One defined indecency only as adultery. Indecency occurred when a wife committed adultery, left her husband for another man, and broke the conjugal bond. In that case, yes, the husband had a legal right to seek a divorce. The other school of thought had a much looser interpretation of indecency. It defined indecency as anything the wife did that the husband didn't like, including burning her husband's food, losing her beautiful figure, or talking so loudly in the home that people could hear her in the street!

The religious leaders were really asking Jesus, "Which interpretation of indecency do you endorse?" Jesus went back to God's original plan for marriage (Matthew 19:4-6). He explained that marriage is not a human institution. God created the marriage institution when He created the first male and female. We don't have the right to tamper with it. The joining of a couple is a divine thing.

They didn't like Jesus' answer, so they pressed the point: "Then why did Moses say that you *could* get divorced?" (v. 7) Jesus explained that God allowed divorce because of the hardness of people's hearts, not because it's desired by God.

If you had a son, your intent would be for that son to submit to you, to love you, to stay pure, and to marry wisely. That would be in his own best interest, as well as pleasing to God. But suppose that son is rebellious and begins to engage in immoral acts. In a fit of anger, he leaves your home. What would you say to him? You might say: "Son, I hope you will stay morally pure. But if you don't, make certain you take precautions. AIDS is killing people by the thousands."

If some people were to overhear, they might question your morality. They might want to know why you're recommending that your son take precautions. But you aren't, really. Your best advice is for him to remain a virgin. But since you know he isn't likely to listen to you, you want him to do the next best thing. You love him and want him to protect himself from disease and death.

Divorce was God's precaution to prevent bad situations from becoming worse. His desire is monogamy forever in a loving relationship. But to a nation with an unrepentant heart, He gave two stipulations for divorce: "You can't do it quickly, and you can't do it flippantly and without cause."

If the religious leaders had looked beyond the Deuteronomy passage about "indecency" to other Old Testament passages (Malachi 2:16, for example), they would have seen clearly that God hates divorce. And Jesus was just as clear: "I say to you, whoever divorces his wife, save for immorality, and marries another commits adultery" (Matthew 19:9).

People disagree on their interpretations of Jesus' statement. Some say the term "immorality" is only used in the gospel of Matthew and is written specifically to the Jews who might need to deal with the violation of a betrothal in a pre-marital relationship. Others say the word clearly refers to adultery. Therefore, divorce and remarriage, except in cases of adultery, is wife swapping, and Jesus does not permit it.

I subscribe to the predominant school of thought among evangelicals: immorality means marital adultery. If someone commits immorality and abandons his mate, the marriage bond is broken. The best course is reconciliation, but if that doesn't occur, the person who abandons another is not free to remarry because that would constitute wife swapping and adultery. In my understanding, the one who has been abandoned and sinned against is allowed to marry again.

A woman told me, "When I got married, my husband gave me a ring and we signed a marriage certificate. Then he went out and bought burial plots for both of us. Do you know why he did that? Because when we put that ring on, we made a commitment that the one of us who goes first will be buried by the other." That's the kind of faithful commitment more couples need today. No church or nation is stronger than its marriages.

the kingdom's demographics

As children were brought to Him for prayer, the disciples were annoyed and rebuked them. These runny-nosed kids didn't deserve to be with the Master! But Jesus said, "No, do not forbid the children. Bring them to me because heaven belongs to them" (v. 14). Jesus loved children, and He appreciated their simple desire to be with Him and know Him. That desire is contrasted with the next story in Matthew's account.

A man approached Jesus and asked: "Teacher, what good thing must I do that I can obtain eternal life?" (v. 16) The gospel of Mark tells us this man was a rich, young ruler. In many ways, he was the polar opposite of the simple, needy children. Jesus responded to the man's question with another question and a directive, "Why are you asking me about what is good? There is only One who is good. If you want to enter life, obey the commandments" (v. 17). Jesus answer communicated, "You really don't need to ask this question because you already know the answer."

The young man asked Jesus *which* commandments he should keep. Is getting into heaven like a batting average? Is 7 out of 10 good enough? Jesus started with the commandments that dealt with people: "Do not murder, do not commit adultery, do not steal, do not give false testimony, honor your father and mother, and love your neighbor as yourself." The young man said he had kept all those commandments since his youth. Then he asked what he was still lacking.

Self-righteous people can examine themselves like a jury and declare themselves righteous like a judge, but like the rich, young ruler, they never have the security in their hearts that they are truly righteous. This young man had been his own jury and his own judge. But it doesn't matter what the criminal thinks about himself; he needs to hear from an impartial party, the judge himself.

Jesus told him, "If you wish to be complete, go and sell your possessions, give to the poor, have treasure in heaven and follow me" (v. 21).There are several interpretations of this text. Some believe this passage teaches that total commitment to God means giving up everything to others. I don't agree because no one else in the Bible is told to do this. Others say this conversation refers to the keeping of the law. If you want to keep the law and you love God, sell everything you have, give to the poor, and follow the Messiah. That's closer. But I think the best interpretation contrasts this self-sufficient, wealthy man in relation to the weak, needy children in the earlier passage. This passage teaches the twelve what is and isn't acceptable to God. It shows the demographics of heaven: there the population is humble and childlike.

A little child with nothing in his hands can come to God. A repentant sinner can come to God like a child and be received into His kingdom. It doesn't matter how lowly, small, poor, or contemptible the person. But self-righteous people refuse to admit their need. I believe Jesus told the young ruler to sell all his stuff because the man was self-righteous, not because he was materialistic. To the Jewish nation at this time, wealth and righteousness were inextricably related, so in effect, Jesus was asking him to relinquish his religious reputation and accomplishments. The man was speechless. He had been chatty up to that point, but he didn't say a word after Jesus' comments pierced his heart.

Jesus told His disciples, "It is easier for a camel to go through the eye of a needle than for a [self-righteous] rich man to enter heaven" (v. 24).The disciples thought the most wealthy were also the most righteous, so they replied with a logical question:"Then who can be saved?" (v. 25) Jesus made it clear to them that salvation is an act of divine power, not self-achievement.

What does this text mean to people today? Suppose a per-

son lives a self-centered and wasteful life. He has venereal disease, including AIDS, and is going to die within the month. He
has lost all he owns. His parents won't speak to him. During
his life he may have violated every religious standard
there is. But if that person confesses his complete
unworthiness before God, and asks like a child, "Can I come
to You?" then God will gladly receive him into His kingdom.

Contrast this attitude with that of the rich young ruler. He
was not poor in spirit. He deemed himself spiritually wealthy.
He was self-satisfied and felt he had kept the commands of
God. He compared himself to other men, and believed himself
superior. But to his dismay, he was not yet worthy of eternal
life. In the same way, churches should not show partiality. We
should accept any and all—no matter how poor or unlovely,
and we should refuse to be attracted or persuaded by the
wealth and fame of unbelievers.

After Jesus' interchange with the rich young ruler, Peter
noted that, "Maybe *he* wouldn't forsake all, but we have!"
(v. 27) Peter wanted to know what kind of reward they would
receive. Jesus said, "When the Son of Man sits on His glorious
throne, you shall also sit upon twelve thrones
judging the twelve tribes of Israel" (v. 28). Of the twelve,
all but John died martyrs' deaths. But Jesus promised the day
would come when they would inherit "many times as much."
But He cautioned them not to compete for rewards: "Many
who are first will be last, and the last will be first"
(v. 30). What will you and I receive? Many times as much. This
gives us contentment instead of competition, a very valuable
lesson for the twelve... and for us.

an attitude of gratitude

Jesus talked about the question concerning rewards
in His next parable (Matthew 20:1-16). He said that the
kingdom of heaven is like a landowner who went out early
in the morning to hire laborers for His vineyard. He agreed
to pay the laborers a denarius for the day, and put them to

work. But the landowner wanted other laborers, and kept going back to the marketplace at various times during the day, taking all those who wanted to work. The first group of workers knew what to expect because they had a clear agreement with the landowner, but those hired later in the day didn't. They were grateful to have a job since they could find no other work, so they worked with an attitude of thankfulness and appreciation. The first served with a legalistic, demanding attitude; the rest served thankfully.

When evening came, the owner of the vineyard told the foreman to pay the workers. First came those who were hired last, and who had worked for only one hour. The owner was delighted to lavish his goodness on these hard-working, appreciative men and to surprise them with "much." Each one received a denarius—a full day's wage! They were elated! But the group who had worked for three hours also received a denarius. So did those who had worked for six hours. But when he got to those who were hired first, they thought they would receive more because they were comparing themselves to the others. They forgot they worked under a contract. When they received the denarius they had agreed to work for, they grumbled and said, "These last men have worked only one hour, and you have made them equal to us who have borne the burden and the scorching heat of the day" (vv. 11-12). The landowner said, "Take what is yours, and go your way. If I wish to give to the last man the same as you, is it not lawful for me to do what I wish with what is my own? Or is your eye envious because I am generous?" (vv. 14-15) Those who worked under the legal agreement received what the agreement stipulated, but those who worked gratefully experienced the owner's goodness and generosity.

God wants laborers who work with an attitude of appreciation and gratitude, not competitive Christians wanting to appear better than others and get all they can possibly get.

Peter had been with Jesus from the beginning. He had borne the scorching heat and the burden of the day. And he wanted to know, "What's in it for me?" Jesus explained that Peter would have his reward, but shouldn't judge himself in comparison to other people or work in a spirit of competitiveness.

A man who was more than 80 years old once lamented to me that he came to the Lord so late in life. I assured him that God will not compare him to anybody else. God only asks him to be faithful today and for the rest of his life. In fact, Paradise was granted to the thief on the cross who only "served" Christ for a few hours. When a six year old wanted to be baptized, I sat down with him to make sure he understood the gospel. He did, and I said to him, "What a joy to know the Savior at the age of six! You'll be able to serve Him 60 or 70 years!" God will judge each person by his motives and his deeds, not the length of time served.

I know a young man named Chad who, because of a childhood disease, has some great limitations. He lived at home and got a job working in a cafeteria. His first job was bussing tables; later he moved up to pouring water and tea. And he didn't just pour your tea, he ran reconnaissance on your table! You'd take a sip, and there he was watching you! "Can I get you some more tea, sir?" Chad was promoted to the service line, and he was pumped! His eyes would catch yours, as he waved his tongs and said with enthusiasm, "Can I get you some bread or toast?" I always got something from Chad. I told my wife, "If I served God with the passion that Chad serves this cafeteria, I would be much better off." Chad counted it a privilege to work and get paid, and he gave everything he had at his job. That's how I want to serve God. Ours is a labor of love! How wonderful it is to work for One who loves us so much!

THE STORY OF GOD   167

Reflection/discussion questions

1. Have you ever been confronted because of your sin? If so, how did you respond? What was the ultimate outcome? How would you respond differently today?

2. Have you seen church discipline practiced? Was the Matthew 18 process followed? What was the outcome? What could have been done differently—and perhaps more effectively?

3. When should you confront someone, and when should you "just let it pass"?

4. How might the confronter's attitude and tone affect the sinner's response?

5. Are you a "good forgiver" when people offend you? Why or why not?

6. How would gaining a better grasp of Christ's forgiveness affect your willingness to forgive others?

7. After reading Jesus' explanations of marriage, hard-heartedness, and divorce, when do you think divorce is appropriate?

8. Who are the "greatest" servants you've ever known? How did they affect most people? How did they affect you?

Chapter 14

THE atonement:
THE pinnacle of time

The attention of the gospels now shifts to the atonement. The entire Bible points to Matthew, Mark, Luke and John because of the focus on Jesus. Prior to the gospels, the Bible anticipates the Messiah's coming. After the gospels, it explains what the Messiah did. The book of Revelation waits for Him to come back. The pinnacle of the Bible is one Man's birth and life. He lived 33 years. Of those 33 years, He only had three years of public ministry. Thirty percent of the pages of the gospels focus on the last week of Jesus' life, and most of that centers on the final six hours of His life at Calvary.

A crossless Christ is heresy. Many liberals teach Christ was merely a historical figure. Many American churches are apostate and present "Christianity" as only a lifestyle modeled by Jesus that we should emulate. They claim Jesus was a good man who suffered and died unjustly, but they discount the supernatural nature of Christ's atonement and resurrection. Paul wrote about people who believe this way: "For there are many who walk, of whom I told you and now tell you even weeping, that they are enemies of the cross of Christ" (Philippians 3:18).

The writers of the gospels don't allow for that view. Jesus' life, words, and behavior do not save people. They do show the perfection and sinlessness of that Person. But it is Christ's death, the atonement, that is the payment for sin. The righteousness God gives me is not due to the life of "a good man"; it is due to the atoning death of a divine sacrifice who alone met the requirements of the Law and now enables God to impart righteousness to all who believe.

ten facts

Let's examine ten things Christ's atonement accomplished that are key to understanding the sovereignty of God. These ten facts show what His death did for God, for us, for history, for Israel, and for the entire physical creation. They will also show what His death did to Satan.

1. *The death of Jesus "propitiates" the wrath of God.*
Propitiation means "to satisfy the wrath of a deity." God forgives because Jesus Christ propitiated, or satisfied, God's wrath.

Isaiah prophesied that "God was pleased to bruise" the Messiah (Isaiah 53:10). Romans 3:25 states, "God displayed Christ publicly as a propitiation in his blood through faith. This was to demonstrate His righteousness."

A prairie fire raged out of control and swept toward a man. He couldn't run; he couldn't hide; he couldn't put out the fire. So he lit a match and set fire to the grass around his feet. It began to burn outward, forming a ring around the man. The raging prairie fire swept past him, and the man was not burned. You see, fire can't burn the same thing twice. Jesus Christ took on our sins and "burned" on Calvary, experiencing the wrath of God. Those who are "in Him" will never feel the wrath of God. Christ's first purpose in dying was not for us. It was for God, so God could be free to act for us.

2. *Jesus' death on the cross demonstrated God's love.*

Paul said it like this: "One will hardly die for a righteous man, though perhaps for a good man someone would dare to die. But God demonstrates His love toward us in that while we were sinners, Christ died for us" (Romans 5:7-8). It's not too hard to conceive of someone dying to rescue a righteous or good person. But it's almost impossible to imagine someone willing to give up his own life for a rebellious and ungrateful enemy. The only one who will do that is God.

When the Bible says, "God demonstrates His love," the Greek word for "demonstrate" means "to stand with" or "to introduce." If I were to introduce you to a group of people, I would stand with you and say, "I want you to meet my friend, so and so." When Jesus came to earth, God stood with Christ and introduced to us a unique love. No one has ever loved to that degree. A great preacher said, "Beyond Calvary, even God cannot go. At last it is shown: 'God is love.'" God is love; the cross is the demonstration of His love.

3. *God's law was established.*

The purpose of Old Testament law was never to save us. No one can meet the demands of keeping the perfect law of God. Even under the law, faith was the basis of a relationship with God: "The just shall live by faith." The purpose of the law was as a tutor to lead us to Christ, to show us our sin, and to direct our eyes to forgiveness at Calvary. "The wages (or the soldier's pay) of sin is death." The penalty of law was finally appeased in the death of Christ.

In the Old Testament, God's presence resided in the temple. People could not approach God except through one designated person, a high priest who presented the shed blood of an animal on a special occasion, the day of atonement. A certain man approached God on a certain day, in a certain way, with a certain sacrifice. So the picture of Old Testament law does not suggest it is something expected of each person. The law simply foreshadowed the death of Jesus Christ.

Why did Jesus Christ have to die? It allowed God to open His arms and receive people who had previously been separated from Him because of sin. And it freed God to be able to confer upon believers all of the benefits of heaven.

4. The atonement defeated Satan.

During the time of the Roman Empire, whenever the army was victorious, they paraded their conquered enemies through the streets for everyone to see. The captives were stripped and marched in humiliation before chariots. Paul referred to this practice when he wrote about Christ's victory over Satan and the demons: "When he had stripped the rulers and the authorities [the demonic realm], He made a public display of them, having triumphed over them through [Christ]" (Colossians 2:15). The ultimate destruction of Satan is described in Revelation 20 when Christ casts him into the Lake of Fire after being bound for a thousand years.

Calvary completely defeated Satan. "The ruler of this world has been cast out" (John 12:31). Jesus said, "One comes into a strong man's house and binds the strong man and strips away his armor and then plunders his possessions" (Luke 11:22). That's what Jesus did. The virgin birth was the Son of God entering into the strong man's house. The cross was the binding of the strong man, and now, Jesus has plundered Satan's possessions—you and me. Christ has freed us from Satan's grasp so we can serve the living God, and someday He shall crush him.

5. The death of Christ redeemed (paid for) the just demands of sin.

The word "redemption" comes from a word that means "the market." When the word is used in the New Testament, it usually means Jesus paid in the marketplace the legal price for sin.

When I share the gospel with someone, I often draw two cliffs. Between the cliffs I draw some fire, and I write over the fire, "judgment, death, and sin." On one cliff I draw a man. Across the great chasm, on the other side is God. He is holy and separated from us by the chasm of sin. Next to God I write, "joy, eternal life, and glory." On the other side, next to man, I write "sin, judgment, and death." I then draw a bridge or two which don't make it across the chasm. I explain that these are bridges man tries to build to get across that gap on his own: going to church, being good enough, giving money to the poor, or helping little old ladies across the street. I ask if the bridge of man's good works can go across that chasm. People generally say something like, "Not enough lumber." And I reply, "You're exactly right." Everything man tries falls short. Then I draw a cross to bridge that gap. On the cross, I spell out the person's name. I tell him that we deserve to be in the fire, but instead God gave us Christ as a bridge. I quote, "He cancelled out the certificate of debt, consisting of decrees against us which were hostile to us. He has taken it out of the way, having nailed it to the cross" (Colossians 2:14). I cross out the person's name, and above it I write "Jesus." I explain that Jesus was nailed to that cross for him. Then, I draw that man crossing the bridge. On the other side, I draw a man standing with God. That's what Christ did for us! He paid the price! He is the bridge to God!

Years ago in the Russian empire, Nicholas, the second Czar of Russia, visited an army outpost. He came upon a soldier who was sleeping. On that man's desk was a loaded revolver and a suicide note. The czar quietly read the note and discovered that this man had been embezzling from the army. Because of gambling debts, he had stolen money, and his theft was about to be revealed to the army. His shame drove him to contemplate suicide, so he wrote a note and put his revolver next to him before he dozed off to sleep. The soldier awoke, planning to end his life, but he noticed that someone had crossed out the note and written below it, "Debts paid by the King of Russia." Now that's what salvation is! A person is condemned and waiting for judgment, but below his or her name appear the words, "Debts paid by the King of Heaven." That's why a believer has the assurance of everlasting life.

6. *The death of Christ reconciled us to God.*

To reconcile means to restore peace, or literally, "to change back." Reconciliation is restoration as if nothing had ever been wrong. Christ "reconciled us in His fleshly body through death to present us before God, holy and blameless and beyond reproach" (Colossians 1:22).

When you have a fight with your spouse, how do you reconcile it? The offender comes to the offended and says, "I am sorry," and there is forgiveness. That's what happens in my home. My wife comes to me, and in the benevolence of my person, I forgive her. (OK, the truth is that I usually go to her and she forgives me!) But that's not the way you and I are reconciled to God. We were not reconciled to God because we went to Him and said we were sorry. Rather, "While we were yet enemies, we were reconciled to God through the death of His Son" (Romans 5:10). The offender didn't do anything. The offended One initiated the reconciliation and sent His Son to the cross where He was put to death by the offenders. He then helped the offenders see their need, and He forgave them based upon His undeserved death. We did nothing.

If you have trusted Christ, you are reconciled and are entitled to be treated as such. God doesn't stick you off in a corner and say, "My Son had to die to save you. Now just sit there and be quiet until the Rapture!" No, He treats you as loved and forgiven. Too often people say they forgive us, yet continue to treat us like dirt. But God's forgiveness is complete. He treats us as forgiven, beloved children.

7. *The believer receives an advocate.*

"If anyone sins," John wrote, "we have an advocate with the Father, Jesus Christ the righteous" (I John 2:1). In high profile trials, the defendant usually has a fleet of lawyers to defend him. The defendant doesn't say a word. The lawyers, the advocates, stand up and plead his case to prove he is not guilty. But our heavenly Advocate does not plead our righteousness. Christ doesn't deny the devil's accusations against us—because they are true! Instead, He pleads His righteousness on our behalf.

Do you remember Perry Mason? It always looked like Hamilton Burger had him until the last five minutes of the show. But rest assured, before the Folgers' commercial, Perry would stand up and point a finger at the real criminal. That is not how our Advocate works. His word to the Father is, "Yes, it's true. Tom did everything Satan accuses him of doing. However, I died in Tom's place, and I am righteous." Because Jesus is our advocate, God sees us as spotless, blameless, without reproach, and we stand secure in that blameless position.

8. Christ acts as a sympathetic high priest.

The writer of Hebrews said Jesus is "not a priest who cannot sympathize with our weakness, but one that has been tempted in all things as we are, yet without sin" (Hebrews 4:15). Let me give you this picture. There are two gardens in the Bible: the Garden of Eden and the Garden of Gethsemane. There are two men: Adam and Christ. There are two trees: the Tree of Life and the cross. One said, "Not thy will but mine be done," and was driven from the Tree of Life. The other said, "Not my will but thine be done," and embraced the cross. Christ obeyed until death. He experienced suffering, rejection, and death. He wept in His distress. Jesus was not estranged from the pains and weaknesses we experience. He knows our hurts and hopes because He has been touched by our infirmities. His life and death were passionate, not mechanical.

When I was a little boy my grandmother died. I loved my grandmother very much. It was the first death I ever experienced. I can remember the strangeness of the

THE STORY OF GOD   175

weeping at the funeral. Do you know what took me through that funeral? My hero was Johnny Unitas, the quarterback of the Baltimore Colts. I had read his autobiography about 63 times! I knew it by heart. When he was a little boy, a loved one died, and he went through that funeral. As I sat through my grandmother's funeral, I comforted myself with the thought that I was sitting in the chair my hero sat in. If Johnny made it, I could make it, too.

Jesus will be with us no matter what we are going through. We can call to Him and receive His strength. He is there to encourage us. Think of the things that are distressing you right now, and remember: "Do not fear. Do not anxiously look about you, for I am your God. I will strengthen you. I will uphold you with My righteous right hand" (Isaiah 41:10).

9. *In Jesus, Israel received its promised Davidic king, and history will end in glory.*

In II Samuel 7, God promised David, "From your loins I will bring forth a king who will rule over the throne, the house, the kingdom of David forever and forever." This King obeyed God completely, and thus He could be raised from the dead, demonstrating that He was the Messiah. He sat down at the right hand of God, and earth has the promise of a monarch, a Davidic King. All of God's purposes to Israel will be fulfilled in Jesus' Second Coming as He will rule a reborn and obedient nation. He will also reconcile human history in Christ. Then, "Every knee shall bow of those who are in heaven and on earth and under the earth, and every tongue shall give praise to God" (Philippians 2:10-11). Jesus Christ is the Davidic king who will reign forever and ever.

10. *The entire physical universe is affected by Christ's atonement.*

When sin occurred, it spread like a red dye covering creation. As death spread to nature, the earth brought forth thorns and thistles. Paul relates the death of Christ to the res-toration of creation in Romans 8: "The creation will some day be set free from its slavery to corruption into the freedom of the glory of the children of God. The whole creation groans and suffers like a woman about to give birth" (Romans 8:21-22).

Someday Christ will come again. As we sing at Christmas, "No more let sin and sorrows grow, or thorns infest the ground. He comes to make His blessings flow, far as the curse is found." Some day after history is completed, Israel fulfilled, evil judged, and death put under Christ's feet, then the entire universe "shall pass away with a roar, and new heaven and new earth will be created where righteousness dwells" (II Peter 3:13). God will accomplish this because of the redemption of Jesus Christ. His death affected God, man, Satan, history, and all creation. Jesus will remove sin, root and branch, in every nook and cranny of creation.

Reflection/discussion questions

1. A person's appreciation for Christ's atoning sacrifice is directly related to his view of his own sinfulness. In what ways does our society communicate that "man is basically good" and only needs minor adjustments, instead of sinful and deserving God's righteous wrath?

2. Restate Romans 5:8 in your own words: "But God demonstrates his own love for us in this: While we were still sinners, Christ died for us."

3. Christ is our friend, our advocate, our high priest, and our king. What do each of Christ's roles mean to you?

4. What would your life—and your future—be like if you had not embraced Christ's atonement?

Chapter 15

THE

CHURCH AGE

I f you drive through Colorado and look at the Rockies, two mountain peaks may appear to be side by side. As you drive closer, however, you find a great valley between the mountains. This valley is like the church age in Scripture: a period between the two peaks of Christ's first and second comings. Between the cross and the crown is the valley of the church, which was not fully explained in the Old Testament. From the perspective of Old Testament passages about the Messiah, the sufferings and the eternal glories of Christ often seem to be simultaneous. These passages didn't depict the valley, the period of the church. The church is the parenthesis in the work of God in the nation of Israel.

The church is an established institution in our country, but many believers do not understand the scope or purpose of this period of biblical history. The church is the New

Covenant promised to Israel in Jeremiah 31:31-33. God promised Israel that someday it would have a new, fresh relationship with Him. In this covenant, external rules give way to an internal desire to obey God as the law is written on people's hearts. This is a "rebirth." The church is not the nation of Israel, but it is "grafted into the rich root of the olive tree" (Romans 11), and it shares in Christ, Israel's Messiah.

God's purposes for the church

The church's primary purpose is to worship God. The second purpose is to "guard the treasure" of the gospel (II Timothy 1:13-14) which has been entrusted to believers. The church protects and defends the Bible and its sacred revelation of salvation. The church's third purpose is "to proclaim the excellencies of Him who called us out of darkness into His marvelous light" (I Peter 2:9). Believers carry the wonderful, life-changing message of the gospel to the entire world. We start in our backyards, and proceed to the most remote corners of the globe. Missions are a vital part of the mandate of the church. Another purpose of the church is to model God's love to people. People long for peace between family members, races, and nations. In Christ's kingdom, believers will serve together "shoulder to shoulder," but until that day, the church is to provide a glimpse of that unity and love. As individuals are transformed by God, they learn to love each other "without distinction between Greek and Jew, circumcised and uncircumcised, barbarian, Scythian, slave and freeman, but Christ is all, and in all" (Colossians 3:11). The love of the body of Christ is the validation of our message to the world.

The miracle of the church is that all people can be one in Christ. Jesus said, "I have other sheep which are not of this fold. I must bring them also, and they shall hear My voice, and they shall become one flock with one shepherd" (John 10:16).

tHe "c's" of dıscıpLesHıp

Discipleship is a major responsibility of the church. New believers are taught and shaped by God's Word to be "equipped for every good deed" (II Timothy 3:17). As this process continues, learners become leaders, and they in turn strengthen others in their *commitment* to God's Word, God's cause, and God's people. They equip others to be *competent* in the know-ledge and application of Scripture to life and ministry. And they are *creative* in ministering to a needy, fallen world.

God's people, the church today, are to be "light and salt" to their culture. Even those who are not converted to Christ will be positively influenced by the holy lives and good works of Christ's people. As light, the church provides truth. As salt, the church prevents spoilage by being the moral restraint in a sinful world.

The church is to care for its own. Many passages in the New Testament encourage us to love, comfort, forgive, accept, stimulate, admonish, serve, teach, restore, and pray for "one another." We are interdependent parts of the body of Christ. We need each other.

The church is a holy institution. At communion, we are advised to "examine ourselves." Baptism is an act of obedience in which we proclaim our death to the old life and our new life in Christ. We also confront sin in our midst so evil will not take root and harm us. We are "children of light" who are called to live holy lives to encourage each other and the world to follow Christ.

LıgHts ın tHe darkness

The *ecclesia* or "called out ones" are to be light "in the midst of a crooked and perverse generation" (Philippians 2:15). We are the kingdom of God which dwells in the kingdom of Satan. Our distinctive, holy influence "destroys speculations and every lofty thing raised up against the knowledge of God, and we are taking every thought captive to the obedience of Christ" (II Corinthians 10:5-6). We are to be obedient sheep in the Good Shepherd's care, servant priests, a holy nation, fruitful branches on the life-giving vine, a faithful bride to a loving groom, and members of the body which are responsive to the head.

Christians have a relationship with a living God who loves, illumines, and leads. We speak of "joining the church," but the term is a bit misleading. Membership requires more than a person's desire to join. Rather, you're born into the church by faith in the Redeemer.

Then Jesus told His followers before His ascension, "All authority has been given to Me in heaven and on earth. Go, therefore, into all the earth, and make disciples of all nations." That was revolutionary! First He told the disciples not to go to the Gentiles. Then He inaugurated an organization which included both Jews and Gentiles. Finally, Jesus told the disciples to aggressively pursue the Gentiles! He told the disciples to teach "all nations" to obey, make disciples of them, and reproduce themselves throughout the globe. And He promised, "Lo, I am with you always, even to the end of the age" (Matthew 28:20), inferring that someday that age would end.

God withholds judgment on this sorry, sin-sick world because He is faithfully gathering His people, His elect, to Himself. When His church is complete, He will act.

Reflection/discussion questions

1. Describe the church's unique place in biblical history.

2. What are some reasons God leaves His church—you and me—here on earth instead of taking us instantly to heaven?

3. Look at a list of "one another" passages in the New Testament. Which of these is your church doing very well? Explain. Which of these is your church doing poorly? Explain. What actions can you take to strengthen your local body of Christ?

Chapter 16

tHe
RaptuRe

For the past 20 centuries, God has patiently gathered His people. During this time, He has tolerated the apathy and rejection of Christ's love by multitudes of people, and He has witnessed the worldwide persecution of the Jewish race. A day will come, however, when God's patience shall be spent, and "the day of the Lord" will come. In that day, He will punish an evil world for renouncing Him at every point in history. And in that day, the nation of Israel will once again take center stage in His divine purposes. That time will come "like a thief in the night." It will begin with an event called "The Rapture."

Certain theologians believe "rapture" is an adoption of a nonbiblical idea. They note the term does not appear in our Bible. The fact is, however, the term appears in the Bible if you have a Latin version. "Rapture" is from the Latin term which means "to grasp or to seize, to take suddenly." Our term "wrap" comes from grabbing something and encasing it. One New Testament passage on the Rapture is I Thessalonians 4:16: "The Lord Himself will descend from heaven with a shout, the voice of the archangel and the trumpet of God, and the dead in Christ shall rise first. Then we who are alive and remain shall be caught up together with them in the clouds to meet the Lord in the air." The phrase "caught up" is translated "rapture" in Latin.

The Rapture and the Second Coming are two different events. The Second Coming will be the visible appearance of Jesus Christ. At that point at the end of the Tribulation, every eye shall see Him at Armageddon when He comes with His church to install His kingdom and to rule the world. The Rapture of the church, prior to the Tribulation, is not visible—at least not to the world—but the church will see Him as we vanish "in the twinkling of an eye." Christ doesn't establish His kingdom at the Rapture. At that point, He comes to remove His people from the earth. "Flesh and blood," Paul said, "cannot inherit the kingdom of heaven." So God changes us as He snatches us away. The purpose of the Rapture is to change the very physical composition of the bodies of the elect "into conformity," Paul said, "with the body of His glory." Also, the Rapture removes believers from the earth in the anticipation of a terrible, cataclysmic event known as the Great Tribulation.

Rapture References

The first mention of the Rapture is from Jesus Himself: "Peace I give unto you. My peace I leave with you, not as the world gives do I give. You believe in God, believe also in me. In my Father's house there are many mansions. I go to prepare a place for you. If it were not so I would have told you. And if I go away to prepare a place for you, I shall come again and receive you unto myself" (John 14:1-3).

Paul developed this doctrine. The Greeks had a saying:

"The doctrine of the resurrection is the doctrine of swine."
To the Greek mind, the physical body was corruptible and
scorned. The higher realities were those of the spiritual and
philosophical realms. (A *platonic relationship* is emotional,
social, and intellectual without becoming physical.) To
combat this error in thinking, Paul assured the Corinthians
that Christ was raised as the first of all His people. Then Paul
explained new truth about the resurrection. He wrote, "I tell
you a mystery. We shall not all sleep (or die), but we shall all
be changed (or resurrected and glorified)." All believers will
be resurrected, but not all will die! That was new news!

Someone told the Thessalonians the persecution they
experienced was the Great Tribulation, but Paul corrected
that mistaken thought. He taught that the dead in Christ
will rise first, then those who are alive will be caught up
together with Him in the clouds to be with the Lord in the
air (I Thessalonians 4:16). All believers, living and dead, will be
changed physically and removed to be with Jesus Christ. This
event is imminent. It could happen tomorrow—or today! The
Second Coming occurs after the Great Tribulation, which is
described in Matthew 24 and Revelation 6-19.

WHAT ARE WE WAITING FOR?

When and why does the Rapture occur? The
Thessalonians believed the intense persecution of their day
was the result of God's judgment. But Paul clarified it for
them: "We wait for His Son from heaven whom He raised
from the dead who delivers us from the wrath to come" (I
Thessalonians 1:10). Is "the wrath to come" a reference to
hell? No, not here. It refers to the Tribulation. There are two
purposes for the Rapture: to prepare us bodily for heaven, and
to remove us from the wrath of God that will be poured out
during the Tribulation.

In the Old Testament, before Sodom and Gomorrah were
consumed, the angel of God said the destruction would not
occur until Lot had been taken from that city. The judgment

of the Flood did not occur until Noah was in the Ark. The fall of Jericho did not take place until Rahab was protected and rescued. The Tribulation is the unveiling of the wrath of God on a wicked world. At that time, the nation of Israel will be brought to its knees to "look on Him whom they have pierced."

Interestingly, the term "church" is not used in Revelation 6-19 because the church is not present during this time. Revelation 4:1 says, "After these things I looked and behold a door standing open in heaven, and the first voice which I heard was like the sound of a trumpet saying, 'Come up here, and I will show you what must take place after these things.'"

A voice calls, a trumpet sounds, and John is instantly in the presence of God. The term, "come up here," is used again in Revelation 11 in connection with the physical "catching away" of the two witnesses in Jerusalem. Prior to the Tribulation in chapter 6, the Rapture takes place. John describes the scene in heaven: "Around the throne were 24 thrones, and upon the thrones I saw 24 elders sitting, clothed in white garments, golden crowns on their head." They are sitting because their work is over. Who are these people? There's only one time in the Old Testament the number 24 is mentioned. King David numbered the priesthood into 24 different orders. I believe the Revelation passage refers to 24 elders, the representatives of a greater mass of people. They represent the church—those who truly know Jesus Christ. They are the ones who are faithful until death, kings and priests who are seated because their work is finished, and they are in heaven.

During the Great Tribulation (Revelation 6-19), men ask for the mountains to fall upon them. Plagues, earthquakes, and disasters of all kinds occur. Christ eventually returns to earth, but He returns with someone: His bride. Verse 7 states, "Let us rejoice and be glad and give glory to Him; because the marriage of the Lamb is come and His bride hath made herself ready." The bride of Christ is the church. We even get a glimpse of her glory: "And it was given to her to clothe herself in fine linen, bright and clean, for her fine linen is the righteous deeds of the saints" (v. 8).

Believers' deeds will be evaluated after the Rapture and before the Second Coming at a judgment seat (*Bema*). Those deeds are rewarded, the saints receive resurrection bodies, and the bride is glorious! Verse 14 records, "The armies which are in heaven, clothed in fine linen, white and clean, were following him on white horses." Again we see people in "fine linen"—identical to verse 8. Who is this who comes with Jesus Christ? It is His bride, the church, in heaven with Him. She isn't on earth when He returns!

Prior to the Tribulation, the Rapture "catches away" a group of people. At the Second Coming of Christ, this group of people returns. They are not on the earth from Revelation 6 to 19. They are in heaven with Christ.

Look at Daniel 9:24-27. If you can understand these four verses, you can comprehend the essence of biblical prophecy. Daniel wanted to know when God's people could go home. The angel didn't answer that question. Instead he told when the final kingdom would come: not at the end of 70 *years*, but at the end of 70 *weeks of years*. "Seventy sevens have been decreed for you and your people and your holy city" (v. 24). The Word of God would be fulfilled at that point, and all of Israel's rebellion would be over. Seventy weeks of years; 70 times seven. That's 490 years.

At the end of that 490-year period, we're going to be in the kingdom. So when does that countdown begin? Verse 25 gives us a clue: "So you are to know and discern from the issuing of a decree to restore and rebuild Jerusalem."

Every Old Testament Jew could tell you the date when the Persian king issued a decree that the Israelites could return to their land. In the books of Ezra and Nehemiah, the nation of Israel returned to restore and rebuild Jerusalem. The decree was issued on March 4, 444 (or 445) B.C. That's when this 490-year period started.

Verse 25 states, "You are to know and to discern from

the issuing of a decree to restore and rebuild Jerusalem until Messiah the Prince comes, there will be seven weeks and 62 weeks." It took about 49 years (seven weeks of years) to rebuild Jerusalem. Seven weeks plus 62 remaining weeks equals 69 weeks of years.

From the issuing of a decree until the time Messiah comes, there were to be 69 weeks of years, or 483 years. Let's begin at 444 B.C. and consider that a Jewish year is only 360 days. Four hundred eighty three years later on the Hebrew calendar is, to the day, the Friday in 33 A.D. when Jesus Christ rode into Jerusalem on a colt. From the issuing of a decree to restore and rebuild Jerusalem to Messiah the Prince, there were supposed to be 483 years. And it happened! The first time I learned this in seminary, I remember sitting in class and looking at my Bible. I thought to myself, "This book really is the Word of God!"

What would Israel do with their king? "Then after the 62 weeks Messiah will be cut off" (v. 26). They're going to kill Him! They're going to nail Him to a cross, pierce His hands and feet, beat him, put thorns on His brow, shoot dice for His possessions, strip Him naked, pierce His side, and leave Him with nothing. "And the people of the prince who is to come will come and destroy the city and the sanctuary." The "prince who is to come" refers to the Antichrist. In 70 A.D. after Israel had rejected Jesus, Jerusalem was attacked by Titus and the Roman legion. They fulfilled prophecy by not leaving one stone of the temple upon another (Matthew 24:2).

Scripture goes on to say, "Its end will come with a flood, and even to the end of time there will be war and desolations" (Daniel 9:26). Jerusalem was destroyed in 70 A.D. This prophecy became fact. In the past 1900 years, Israel has experienced a "flood" of desolations and war, just as Daniel predicted.

tHe missinG week

Seventy "sevens" were decreed, after which the Messiah's kingdom will come. But we're missing something—one of the

70 weeks. The Messiah came after 69 weeks of years, and then it was as if God called a timeout. We're missing the 70th week that Daniel spoke of: one more seven-year period.

The book of Revelation focuses on a seven-year period when the nation of Israel is broken. Daniel 9:27 refers to this 70th week: "And he [the Antichrist] will make a firm covenant with the many [Israel] for one week." We're still waiting for this week to take place.

Incidentally, this prophecy assumed that some day the nation of Israel would exist as an entity that could physically and politically make a covenant with a man. I can speak on this topic with assurance today, but I wonder what I would have thought in 200 A.D. or 1000 or 1850 or 1945 when there was no physical nation of Israel. In those days, it must have been difficult to adhere to a literal interpretation of the books of Daniel and Revelation.

But in 1948 the modern nation of Israel was formed. The "bones" of Ezekiel's vision gathered together into a great army, "though they have no life" (Ezekiel 37). Yet now that they have done so, Daniel tells us they will make a covenant with a pagan man which they would not make with Jesus Christ.

Then Daniel continues, "But in the middle of the week, he will put a stop to sacrifice and grain offering and on the wing of abominations will come one who makes desolate" (9:27). Again, this reference to sacrifices assumes there will be a temple and a priesthood—sure signs of a restored Israel. The reference to "the middle of the week" also lets us know there will be significance to a three-and-a-half year period sometime in the future.

The Antichrist will someday take his seat in the temple of God, displaying himself as God (II Thessalonians 2:4). There is no temple today, but at some point after it is erected the Antichrist will betray the nation of Israel and persecute them severely. Yet this persecution will end when, as the last clause of Daniel 9:27 states: "one that is decreed is poured out on the one who makes desolate." Christ will come, and He will destroy the Antichrist by the word of His mouth (II Thessalonians 2:8).

How does this text relate to the Rapture of the church? The church is raptured to raise the saints and remove them from the wrath of God to come. This occurs prior to the Tribulation. The Tribulation period is not a church dispensation; it is the fulfillment of God's plan for Israel. Keep Israel and the church distinct in your theology.

At this point in history we're in "the mystery" between verses 26 and 27 of Daniel 9, when Israel's Messiah and Israel's covenant have been extended to the Gentiles (Romans 11:25 and II Peter 3:8-9). The wrath of God has been postponed until God gathers "the fullness of the Gentiles." And then, "All Israel will be saved, for the deliverer will come from Zion and remove sin from Jacob. This is my covenant with them when I take away their sin."

"chicken doctrine"?

Some people suggest that the interpretation of a pre-tribulation Rapture is a "chicken doctrine." I don't agree. God's people should be willing to suffer and die for Christ. But my position on the pre-tribulation Rapture makes sense as long as we understand the difference between Israel and the church. The Tribulation is a Jewish dispensation from God.

If you are not a Christian, please pay special attention first to these historic events:

1. God predicted the decree to restore and rebuild Jerusalem and it came true.
2. He predicted the razing of Jerusalem after 483 years, and it came true.
3. He predicted the coming of Christ, and He came.
4. He predicted the Messiah would be cut off, and it came true.
5. He predicted the sanctuary would be destroyed, and it happened.

6. He predicted there would be desolations to the end, which we see throughout the world every day.
7. He predicted that someday there would be a gathering of Israel, and it has come true.

All that is left is for an Antichrist to make a covenant with Israel, after which will come the greatest tribulation the world has ever known. Since God has been right on target up till now, don't you think there's at least an outside chance He'll be correct about the rest of what is to happen? In this period of time while the storm clouds are gathering, while the wrath of God has been expended toward His Son who died for sin but delayed toward this wicked earth, I urge you to enter the ark of faith while there is still time! The wrath of God is not something you want to experience!

reflection/discussion questions

1.   What are the differences between the Rapture and the Second Coming?

2.   Describe these aspects of the Rapture:

     the dead in Christ:
     those who are alive:
     being with Christ in the air:
     the transformation of our bodies:
     the purpose of the Rapture:

3.   Are you ready for the Rapture right now, today? Why or why not?

4.   Complete this sentence: I'm looking forward to the Rapture because. . .

Chapter 17

THE JUDGMENT SEAT
OF CHRIST

The Olympic games began in Athens as a way for the best athletes to compete. Athletes made a vow to keep all of the rules for a year. They had a regimen of diet, morality, and training. If athletes could not keep this vow, they were not allowed to win the prize. Before the prizes were awarded, all the participants stood in front of a judgment seat where they swore before Caesar that they had competed according to the rules. This judgment seat was called "the Bema."

The apostle Paul witnessed these events and used this concept to illustrate the Christian judgment: before a reward is given to the Christian, there is a judgment. The judgment is not to punish sin, but rather to acknowledge accomplishments for Christ. The New Testament mentions this judgment seat at least ten times. This will occur after the Rapture and before Christ's Second Coming.

In a Jewish wedding, a man betroths himself to a woman, then the woman beautifies herself in preparation for her wedding day. When everything is ready, the bridegroom comes to take his bride away to the wedding festivities. The first thing they do is consummate their marriage in the bridal chamber. Then they appear to all the people invited to the wedding feast, and a new family is established. That's a beautiful picture of the Christian who is "in Christ." We have been betrothed to Him by faith, and we have been given the Holy Spirit as a token of what is to come (like an engagement ring). Right now we should be getting ready and preparing ourselves for His coming. He will take us to glory where we will be with Him. Then we will appear with Him at the wedding supper in His kingdom.

I've never seen an ugly bride. (I've seen dozens of ugly grooms, but who's looking at them anyway?) Christ will soon come to get us, and we will go away with Him. These days, women either buy or make their bridal gowns, but the church receives hers from Christ.

Most of us don't want to hear about judgment in any shape or form. Yet "judgment" for Christians is something we should look forward to. We will not be judged for sin. In the death of our Lord, God has taken our sins and separated them from us "as far as the east is from the west." He has placed them in a divine forgetfulness through the blood of Jesus Christ, and we are seen as righteous. However, "we shall all appear before the judgment seat of Christ" (II Corinthians 5:10). Romans 14:12 states, "Each of us shall give account of himself to God." The writer to the Hebrews said, "All things are laid bare before the eyes of Him to whom is our accounting" (Hebrews 4:13).

After false teachers at Corinth charged Paul with having self-seeking motives to elevate himself, he spent five chapters explaining that his motives as a minister of the New Covenant were pure. He summarizes his lengthy defense by writing, "We have as our ambition, whether at home or absent, to be pleasing to Him, for we must all appear before the judgment seat of Christ that each one may be recompensed for his deeds in

the body according to what he has done, whether good
or bad. Therefore, knowing the fear of the Lord, we
persuade men" (II Corinthians 5:9-10). Paul's motives
were pure because he kept in mind his coming "judgment."
He had a passion to please God and the wisdom to fear Him.

Peter said, "If you regard as father the one that impartially
judges according to each man's work, conduct yourself in
fear" (I Peter 1:17). God will judge us, so we relate to Him in
reverence. Being a Christian lets you escape hell, but you will
still experience the believer's judgment. The purpose is not
punishment but accountability so that "each man's praise"
will come from God for what we have done.

YOUR day In couRt

Let's examine some aspects of the believer's judgment:

1. It is inclusive: we *all* appear. "Appear" means "to make
    manifest." Something that was unseen is now visible.
2. It is individual.
3. The judgment is not for sin.
4. We are judged for our deeds.

You may be thinking, "I've worked in the secular world
all my life. I guess my judgment will be pretty bleak!" Or if
you are in the ministry, you might be tempted to think, "I've
worked for God for 45 years. What a wonderful judgment this
will be for me!" But as one theologian said, "The judgment
seat of Christ is not so much about *what* you have done, but
why you did what you did: What was your motive?" That's
why II Corinthians 5:10 states the purpose of this judgment
is according to deeds in the body, "good or bad."

The Greek word at the end of verse 10 literally means
"light" (the opposite of "heavy"). We'll be judged for what
we've done, literally, "whether good or light." This implies we
either live for the weightier things of God's glory, or we live
for our own exaltation, which will perish when we do. In

Hebrew, the word for "glory" is the same as the word "heavy." The glory of God was seen as a heavy, or permanent, thing. In reference to the glory of man, the Psalms say of the wicked, "They are like chaff that the wind blows away." We won't be judged according to whether we've been missionaries, preachers, Bible teachers, or Sunday School leaders. Rather, we will be judged according to our deeds and our motives.

This is a great encouragement, especially if you're involved in "secular work" (which is sacred to God if you perform it for His honor). God notices your motives as well as your deeds. And those like me who are in public ministries can see that God is not impressed with our visibility. He will judge *why* we have done what we have done. We are made "manifest before the judgment seat."

At sports banquets, the coach presents the Most Valuable Player awards. These awards tend to go to the most visible players: the running back who had 120 yards per game, the quarterback who threw for two touchdowns a game, or the point guard who scored 30 points per game. But a good coach may surprise everyone by giving the award to a 140-pound, second-string nose guard who got beat up every day in practice but gave all he had to the team. The coach sees beyond what the people at the game see. He sees clearly.

I once gave an invocation at a Chamber of Commerce banquet. Later an award was announced, which was followed by a spontaneous, happy response from the crowd. The woman who was named had worked tirelessly in the background, and she was faithful in everything she did. Everyone was so happy she was honored. As soon as her name was called, she broke down in tears because she never thought she would be recognized in this way. She simply did the best she could... where she was...in her own small way. That's what the judgment seat of Christ is all about.

work that matters

Paul wrote: "Do your work heartily as for the Lord rather

than for men, knowing it's from the Lord that you will receive the recompense of the inheritance" (Colossians 3:23-24). That admonition is directed to slaves in Colossae, yet it reminds us as well: God sees what you do and how you do it. In Ephesians 6:8, Paul wrote, "Knowing that whatever good each one does, this he will be recompensed from the Lord, whether slave or free." One text on the judgment seat of Christ applies specifically to slaves; the other one applies to all of us.

What does it mean that "we will be recompensed?" We get some additional insight from I Corinthians 3:10-11: "According to the grace of God which was given to me as a wise architect, I laid a foundation and another is building upon it. But let each man be careful how he builds. No man can lay a foundation other than the one laid which is Jesus Christ." The apostle Paul casts himself as an architect who lays a foundation and leaves. Then he subcontracts the building out to other teachers. He warns false teachers who had come into Corinth that they had better be careful how they build. These teachers continued the work Paul had begun, but that work was supported by the strength and truth of the original foundation, Jesus Christ. Their work should then continue to be based on the imperishable Word of God, not on man's philosophy.

Paul continues, "If any man (that is, any teacher) builds upon the foundation with gold, silver, precious stones, granite or marble, wood, hay, straw, each man's work will become evident" (v. 12). "Become evident" is the same word used in II Corinthians 5:10 for, "We shall all appear," or "be manifest." This word means that the true character of the person or thing is exposed. At the Bema, each man's work will be shown for what it really is.

Right now, many works and motives are hidden. The church often applauds people who appear worthy but are not truly good. On the other hand, great men and women frequently go unnoticed. But that's okay, because "we shall *all* be made manifest." On the day when the lights come on, darkness is dispelled, and we are caught up in the presence of Christ, people's deeds will be revealed with fire. This fire will test the quality—not the amount—of each person's work.

Paul wrote, "If any man's work which he has built upon it remains, he shall receive a reward." This promise is addressed specifically to teachers to taught God's Word. Their efforts, Paul says, will be rewarded by God.

Paul then deals with the flip side: "If any man's work is burned up, he shall suffer loss, but he himself will be saved yet as though through fire." The Christian teacher who communicates error is least in the kingdom of heaven. He has betrayed "the least of these" because he built upon the foundation with error—straw that will be destroyed in the fire of God's judgment. He will certainly "suffer loss."

one last story

What's the "reward" and what's the "loss" that Paul speaks of? Are there levels of heaven? I don't believe so, but there will be different roles in the kingdom. Charles Hodge, a great Bible commentator in the 1800s, said of a person who experiences "loss" because of his deeds, "He will occupy a lower place in the kingdom of heaven than he would have done."[1] Now where did Hodge get that idea?

Luke 19 records the last words spoken by Jesus Christ prior to going to die. Jesus told a parable because they were near Jerusalem, and the disciples supposed the kingdom of God was going to appear immediately. The disciples saw the coming of Christ and His ruling over the world as simultaneous events. They didn't understand the mystery of the church age.

He told of a nobleman who planned to go to a distant country to receive a kingdom and then return. Before leaving, he called ten of his slaves and gave them ten minas each telling them, "Do business until I come" (Luke 19:12-13).

The phrase "do business" means "make a profit." The word in Greek is the source of our word *pragmatic*. When Jesus left the earth, He equipped IIis followers with what they needed and told them what He expected when He returned. He's a good businessman. He has gone away, but He has left us here to "do business" until He returns. He wants His treasure to increase.

But the parable tells how the people responded to the absentee nobleman: "The citizens hated him." They said, "We will not have this man reign over us." The same is true today: It is difficult to "do business for Jesus" in our culture. People are not excited when we preach the gospel to them. They reject Christ and His holy standards of morality. Jesus continued, "It came about that when he returned, after receiving the kingdom, he ordered that these slaves to whom he had given the money might be called to him to know what they had done. The first appeared and said, 'Master, your mina has made ten minas more.' He said, 'Well done good slave. Because you have been faithful in a very little thing, be in authority over ten cities.' Another responded, 'Your mina, master, has made five minas.' He said, 'You are to be over five cities.'"

Now what does it mean, "ten cities" and "five cities"? I believe these are literal cities over which believers will rule during Christ's kingdom. Others will "suffer loss" and not receive the honor of ruling over any cities. Because I take the literal approach, I believe in a literal coming and a literal kingdom in which "thrones will be set up." I have no problem believing the church will first be judged and then will return with Christ. They will rule with Him. "Blessed are the poor in spirit, for theirs is the kingdom of heaven. Blessed are the meek, for they shall inherit the earth" (Matthew 5:3,5). When Christ sets up thrones, you and I will be there!

Where will you rule? I don't know, but in some way, Christ will delegate His kingdom to all believers throughout history. John wrote, "Beware of what you have received that you might not lose what we have accomplished, but did you receive a full reward?" (II John 8) I think of another text from Paul, "I buffet my body and make it my slave lest after I have called others to the race, I should be disqualified" (I Corinthians 9:27). The loss Paul mentioned is a loss of reward in Christ's kingdom.

WORTH THE WAIT

On two occasions in the Old Testament, David was rejected—once by Saul and again by Absalom. David left the city of Jerusalem as a kind of Old Testament Robin Hood. He lived in the desert and organized men and women who believed the promise of God that he would become king. They chose to suffer and follow David. When David finally became king, immediate judgment fell upon his enemies and his faithful followers were established in authority. A woman by the name of Abigail was willing to marry David when he was still a refugee and outcast because she believed he eventually would receive his kingdom. She married him and was transformed from a pauper to a queen. It's the same with us. We have chosen to follow the rejected Savior, believing that someday He will rule.

Dr. Dwight Pentecost of Dallas Theological Seminary said part of our glory or loss may be of the degree of our eternal glory. He said if you go into a room, a chandelier may illumine that room with 50-watt, 100-watt, and 200-watt bulbs. In the Eternal City full of glory and honor, there will be different "bulbs," some 100-watt Christians, some 50-watt Christians, and some 200-watt Christians.

This concept of believers' judgment doesn't "sit well" with some of us, even though it's mentioned often in the gospels and Paul's letters. Daniel 12:3 says in the eternal day, "Those that had insight will shine brightly like the brightness of the heavens and their expanse, and those that lead the many to righteousness, like stars forever and forever." How brightly will you shine? Will you be a bright lantern or a dim bulb? It's your choice.

Many of us ask God to bless our selfish ambitions. Others, however, have died to ourselves and let God use us to accomplish His work. We have said, "God, I want my tongue to speak for You. Take my marriage, take my children, take my life, and

I'll live it for the weightier things and Your glory." People may not notice, but God does. Someday there will be a judgment seat. Unless we compete according to the rules, we won't receive a prize.

At the back of my house is a woodpile about three feet high, ten feet long, and two feet wide. I use that wood during the winter to warm our home. At the end of the winter, that woodpile is gone. The fire reduces it to its basic state and exposes it for what it was: perishable. As the last act of the winter, I take a grocery bag and a shovel to the fireplace, and that entire half cord of wood is reduced to one shopping bag of ashes. Then I pour these ashes along the hedge as fertilizer. After the first rain, it's as if that wood never existed. This is a picture of what will happen to a lot of Christians. They don't read their Bibles, they don't share the Word of God, and they don't serve Christ. They live for their own glory, their income, their clothing, their houses, their cars, and their majesty. Someday they will go home to be with the Lord, and their deeds and motives will be tested. They have sowed to the flesh, and from the flesh they shall reap decay, ashes, nothing. They lived for man's approval, and they received it. But they forfeited God's approval in the process.

I don't know about you, but I want to devote my life to the great King who someday shall appear. All the commendation I ever need will be, "Well done, good and faithful servant" (Luke 19:17).

Reflection/discussion questions

1. How does the reality of the Judgment Seat of Christ presently affect your goals and behavior?

2. If you appeared before Christ right now and your deeds were tested by fire, would you be happy with the results? Why or why not?

3. What are some specific changes you need to make so that on that day you will hear, "Well done, good and faithful servant?"

    Consider how you relate to:
        family members—
        your private life (thoughts, dreams, etc)—
        affection for God—
        use of time—
        use of money—
        use of possessions—
        goals and desires—
        work—
        ministry—

[1] Charles Hodge, *First Corinthians,*
    (Grand Rapids, Mich.: Eerdmans Publishing, 1950), p. 58.

Chapter 18

THE
TRIBULATION

T here are certain biblical terms that are familiar to almost
everyone. Everybody knows about "The Prodigal Son" and
"The Good Samaritan." Due to secular movies, most people
have at least heard about the Tribulation, the Antichrist, the
Beast, and Armageddon—even though few presentations of
these concepts are biblically accurate. And few people
comprehend the nuances of this period in biblical prophecy.

The Tribulation is prophesied in detail in Revelation 6-19,
but is first mentioned in Deuteronomy 4:30: "When you are
in distress and all these things have come upon you, in the
latter days you will return to the Lord your God and listen to
His voice." Before the nation of Israel responds to the Messiah,
there must be a time of distress. In the same way, before you
were converted, you probably had a time of distress which
showed your need for a Savior.

God told Jeremiah: "Ask now and see if a male can give birth. And yet, why do I see every man with his hands on his loins as a woman in childbirth and all faces have turned pale?" (Jeremiah 30:6-7) The greatest pain a woman experiences is childbirth. The men of the nation of Israel are depicted as going into labor. They are in great pain. The reason is found in verse 7: "Alas! For that day is great, there is none like it. It is the time of Jacob's trouble." The Tribulation will be "the time of Jacob's trouble."

tHe oRdeR of events

Paul describes to the Thessalonians what will happen first. They had been told the day of the Lord had already come, and they were going to suffer through it. Consequently, they were in great turmoil. Paul writes, "I pray that you will not be quickly shaken from your composure or disturbed either by a spirit or a message or a letter as if from us to the effect that the day of the Lord has come" (II Thessalonians 2:1-2). "The day of the Lord" refers to the time of the Tribulation, the period of God's judgment. Paul instructed the Thessalonians not to get shaken up thinking they were in the middle of the Tribulation. Throughout church history, Christians have thought, "This is it! This must be the Tribulation!" During World War II, many believers thought Adolph Hitler was the Antichrist and Benito Mussolini was the False Prophet. Naziism, they believed, was the kingdom of the Beast, the Holocaust was the destruction of the nation of Israel, and the atom bomb fulfilled certain judgments of Revelation. Some people were ready to go on a hilltop and wait for Christ to appear. But it didn't happen. If you're a Christian, you can know when the Tribulation has come: If you're here, it hasn't come yet!

Paul continues, "Let no one deceive you. It will not come unless the apostasy comes first, and the man of lawlessness is revealed" (v. 3). "The man of lawlessness" is the Antichrist, the final embodiment of all of Satan's dreams. One day the Father will enthrone Christ to rule the world and bring religious, political, economic union from Jerusalem. In a mirror image of Christ's coming kingdom, Satan will give all authority to the Antichrist who will institute political, spiritual, and economic union to the world and take his seat in Jerusalem, displaying himself as God in the Temple. Thus he is "anti" Christ, meaning "in the place of" or "against" Jesus Christ.

In verse 6, Paul continues, "You know what restrains him now, so that in his time he may be revealed." In other words, the devil has always wanted to deceive the world and destroy the nation Israel. Satan does not mature in his evil. He has always hated the elect nation of Israel, he has always hated God, and he has always longed to deceive man. But something restrains him: "The mystery of lawlessness is already at work, only he who now restrains will do so until he is taken out of the way."

Who is this "he" who holds back the devil? This person is obviously greater than the devil. Only God can restrain Satan. Jesus said to the apostles, "Satan has demanded permission to sift you like wheat" (Luke 22:31-32). Satan can never act completely independently. This Tribulation and the final period of evil cannot occur until the restrainer of evil is taken out of the way. The restrainer is God's Holy Spirit who works through the body of Christ. The restrainer is taken out of the way when the church is raptured from the earth. Just as the flood came when Noah and his family were safe in the Ark, evil will come when God's people are safely out of the way.

Let's take a closer look at what will happen.

1. *The removal of the church.*

The event that will initiate the Tribulation is the removal of the world's godly, restraining influence—the church. She will be gone, and as a result, "God will send upon them a deluding influence" (II Thessalonians). Just as God hardened Pharaoh's heart in his wickedness to bring about judgment on Egypt and glorify Himself, God will harden the sinful world to bring about His glory and their judgment.

2. *A unified world.*

Next we see something which has not happened since the 5th century A.D. By that time, the world had been ruled by the great kingdoms of Assyria, Egypt, Babylon, Persia, Greece, and Rome. These governments attempted to control the planet. Since the fall of Rome, there has not been another empire. Napoleon tried it. Hitler tried it. Lenin and Stalin tried it. But no one ever succeeded. At the beginning of the Tribulation, however, the books of Daniel and Revelation prophesy a confederacy of kings in Europe. Ten rulers will come together and gain ascendency over the former Roman Empire. Their power, however, is challenged and short-lived because it is weak. Many people believe the European Common Market (or European Economic Community) is—or is the forerunner of—this ten-nation confederacy.

Man has often dreamed that some day the nations would come together and produce righteousness on this earth. This result can be accomplished only through the conversion of the world through Jesus Christ and the obedience of the world to Him.

3. *A man will take control.*

The book of Daniel speaks of "a little horn that uproots" (Daniel 7:8) three of those ten kings. The book of Revelation says the ten kings have come to their power for one purpose, and that purpose is to give their authority to the Beast (Revelation 17:17).

One of the biblical names for pagan government is "a beast," which is a creature with power but no conscience. Heathen world empires are called "beasts," but in Revelation, a particular person is called "the Beast"—not just his empire, but him. "The Beast" is another name for the Antichrist. In history, some nations have given inordinate power to one man. Germany gave it to Hitler. Russia gave it to Joseph Stalin. The United States gave extraordinary power to Franklin Roosevelt during the Depression.

Having a king is no problem as long as he is righteous, but

if you get the wrong fellow in there, you're in trouble!

4. *The Antichrist takes control and introduces a "utopia."*

The Antichrist promotes one-world religion without the true church to oppose him. His False Prophet serves as a combination priest and public relations guru (Revelation 13:11-18). The False Prophet looks like a lamb but speaks like a dragon. He brings about an ecumenical movement, a world church the Bible calls "a harlot" (Revelation 17:1-6), because she is unfaithful to her Sovereign. This harlot is apostate Christianity. With all the saints gone, this Christless, crossless religion will be an amalgamation of all religions. The Antichrist also will establish a one-world commercial system that is called "Babylon the Great" (Revelation 18). In fact, many scholars believe the Antichrist will establish his seat of control in literal Babylon, present-day Iraq, which today is being rebuilt under Saddam Hussein. The Antichrist will appear to do what God could not do: establish a kingdom of peace.

One of the great failures of Israel in the Old Testament was their persistence in making covenants with the Assyrians and the Egyptians. But in the last days, Israel will make a binding covenant with this Gentile, the Antichrist. He will make a covenant with Israel for a seven-year period (Daniel 9:27), and the Antichrist will even allow the Israel to begin temple worship. The political existence of the nation of Israel is central to the Bible's teaching about the Tribulation. From about 70 A.D. until just a few short decades ago, Ezekiel's prediction seemed like far-fetched prophecy, but today, the tiny country of Israel again has center stage in world affairs.

5. *A portion of Israel will be enlightened.*

The fifth event is the enlightenment of Israel. There will be 144,000 Jews who are converted and will become the "first fruits to God and to the Lamb" (Revelation 14:4). They are a new order in the Tribulation. We can't call them "church believers" because there is no church during that time. They are "Tribulation saints" or "completed Jews" who begin to preach the gospel, and they will see a great harvest of Gentiles come to faith (Revelation 7:9-17). The veil will be removed from "144,000 Jewish Billy Grahams." They will see the truth, and they will preach the Word of God.

6. *Two kingdoms unite against the rule of Antichrist.*

Two kingdoms are depicted in great length in Ezekiel 38 and Daniel 11. One is called the King of the North and the other is the King of the South. They attack Israel, which is allied with Antichrist. The King of the North is identified as "the Prince of Rosh" (which is known today as Russia). The Kings of the South are identified as an Egyptian/Arab coalition. As these two powers converge, the Antichrist will aid Israel in its fight against these two kingdoms. But God is the one who will supernaturally destroy the King of the North and the King of the South (Ezekiel 38). The carnage will be so great it will take seven years to bury the dead. These kingdoms are depicted in Joel 2 as a great hoard of locusts which swarms over Israel, but God drives them into the Mediterranean Sea and leaves their carcasses for all to see.

7. *Antichrist breaks his covenant with Israel.*

The Antichrist seizes his opportunity and makes Israel the center point of his kingdom. "He will pitch his tents of his royal pavilion between the seas [the Mediterranean] and the beautiful holy mountain [which is Jerusalem], yet he will come to his end, and none will help him" (Daniel 11:45). He makes Jerusalem the seat of his throne, just like Christ will do in His kingdom. People are awed at the Antichrist's power. They exclaim, "Who is like the Beast? And who is able to wage war with him?" (Revelation 13:4)

But then the Antichrist violates his covenant with Israel. Daniel 9:27b states, "And in the middle of the week (seven-year period), he will break his covenant, and on the wing of abominations, one will come." In II Thessalonians 2:4,

Paul explains that the Antichrist "will take his seat in the temple of God, displaying and exalting himself as God." Daniel's term for this act of blasphemy is the "abomination of desolation" (Daniel 12:11). The same term was used in connection with Greek leader, Antiochus Epiphenes (Daniel 11:31), who asserted his authority over the nation Israel by placing a statue of Zeus in the Holy of Holies and forcing the nation of Israel to worship it.

Jesus Christ said "the abomination of desolation" would appear again (Matthew 24:15). He told the twelve, "When you see this occur, let him who is on the housetop not come down. Don't go back for your cloak, for a time of distress will come upon the world such as has never been seen from its beginning until then" (Matthew 24:16-21). The Antichrist will take his seat in the Temple of God at the midpoint of the seven-year Tribulation.

8. Divine judgments fall on the Antichrist's kingdom.

Some portions of the book of Revelation are mysterious and describe God's direct, supernatural cursing of the earth, its waters, its oceans, its green grass, and its trade. There are cosmological occurrences in the heavens and demonic occurrences in which the inhabitants of the bottomless pit (demonic beings who have been confined from Genesis 6 to that point) are released upon the earth. The judgments during this period are even more horrific than the judgments upon Egypt during the time of Moses. Cecil B. DeMille said, "If it's in the Bible, I can make a movie of it." But I'm not sure even Mr. DeMille could have made one about Revelation! It is too incredible and too bizarre.

9. The Antichrist burns the harlot with fire and sets himself up as deity.

The Antichrist makes the nations of the earth pay homage to him as God, much as Nebuchadnezzar made Shadrach, Meshach and Abednego bow down to him as God. Just as Nebuchadnezzar said, "If you don't worship me, you must die," so this man will proclaim that all must bear his seal upon their heads or arms. His seal is the number 666. In the Bible, the number three represents God, and six represents man. The number 666 probably signifies "man replacing God." Without this seal, people cannot buy or sell goods.

Let me explain a commonly misused passage of Scripture. According to Matthew 25:32, when Christ returns, "He shall gather the nations before Him." He will first address the Gentiles who lived through the Tribulation: "I was hungry and you did not feed me. I was thirsty and you did not give me drink. I was in prison and you did not visit me. I was naked and you did not clothe me." They respond, "Lord, when did we see you hungry, thirsty, in prison, or naked?' And He will say to them, "Whatsoever you did to the least of these my brethren, you did it unto me" (Matthew 25:42-45).

His "brethren" are Jews who would not worship Antichrist and consequently suffered degradation, imprisonment, and death (Revelation 12:13-17). The way that you can tell if a Gentile is truly converted during the Tribulation is by his or her treatment of the Jews. Believing Gentiles will treat the Jews the way Corrie ten Boom treated them during World War II: protecting them and providing for their needs. This passage of Scripture is frequently used to exhort us to care for the poor and needy, but that misses the whole point. The teaching is actually an eschatological text about the judgment of Gentiles who will not care for suffering Jews.

10. *Two godly "witnesses" are the final voice of God to unrepentant Israel.*

One of these godly men will turn the waters into blood, just as Moses did. The other will call fire down on those who oppose him and will shut up the heavens from raining, just as Elijah did. The two great witnesses of the Old Testament were Moses and Elijah, representing the law and the prophets. During this final day, two powerful men will minister in Jerusalem for three-and-a-half years (Revelation 11). Once again, the law and the prophets will call Israel to faith

THE STORY OF GOD

(Romans 3:21). It is debated whether these two men are *like* Moses and Elijah (which I believe), or *are* Moses and Elijah in some kind of resurrection.

These men will be put to death by the Antichrist, and their bodies will be left exposed for a period of time as an act of disgrace. Miraculously, they will come back to life and ascend into heaven as an affirmation of their message about Jesus: He died and rose from the dead and ascended into heaven! At that point, an earthquake occurs in Jerusalem as God's affirmation of the witnesses' words, and the city collapses. God speaks and affirms His Word! This is God's final call to an Israel which is still involved in Old Testament worship in the temple (Revelation 11:1) and who did not recognize Jesus as the Messiah. By this time, the faithful of Israel have fled into the wilderness to be protected by God (Matthew 24:15 and Revelation 12).

11. *Huge armies converge.*

An army in the east of 200 million soldiers will rebel against the rule of Antichrist. They will attack Israel on a plain Napoleon said would be the ideal site of the world's final battle. It is called the "plain of Megiddo," or Armageddon. At this place, the army of the east, along with many other nations, will face the army of Antichrist.

Zechariah 12 describes that last battle on the plain of Megiddo. Verse 2 says, "Behold I am going to make Jerusalem a cup that causes reeling to all the peoples around, and when the siege is against Jerusalem, it will be against Judah." In the Old Testament, judgment frequently is spoken of as drunkenness, or as a cup people drink from. When people get drunk, they reel, fall, and lie prostrate. Someday the cup of reeling will be passed to the nations, and they will be drunk with judgment.

Zechariah continues, "It will come about in that day that I will make Jerusalem a heavy stone." The people will think they can pick up Jerusalem and deport the people, but instead, they will be severely injured. Here's why: "In that day,

I will strike every horse with bewilderment and his rider with madness, but I will watch over the house of Judah." Verse 10 describes how God will care for Judah, His people: "I will pour out on the house of David and on the inhabitants of Jerusalem the spirit of grace and supplication." The Holy Spirit will be poured upon them and produce humility, grace, and supplication.

When a person is converted today, the Spirit produces a spirit of grace and the humility to pray for Christ's forgiveness. Someday, God said, He will work in the hearts of the entire nation of Israel. He will pour out upon them the Spirit of conversion. The nation of Israel will look upon Jesus as the one they pierced, and they will mourn for Him as for an only son. The condition of God's blessing upon the nation of Israel is that the entire nation corporately repents and turns to God (Deuteronomy 31:1-10). The book of Joel says the bride comes out of her bridal chamber (Joel 2:16). She is so overwrought with contrition that she will leave her honeymoon, come to an assembly, and call out for mercy. You're talking about serious repentance when you leave your honeymoon because you're overwhelmed with judgment!

II Chronicles 7:14 records a familiar passage: "If my people who are called by my name will humble themselves and pray and seek my face and turn from their wicked ways, then I will hear from heaven, forgive their sin, and I will heal their land." Israel has never fulfilled this condition even though they were implored by John the Baptist, Jesus, the twelve, and Peter. And they never will fulfill it until God takes them through the Tribulation period and bends them until they break. In that day, a spirit of grace and supplication will be poured out on them. They will "look upon Him whom they have pierced" (Zechariah 12:10), and they will call out to God. This is the nation's last gathering before judgment falls.

The stage is then set for the fifth invader of the nation of Israel. After being confronted by the kings of the north, south, east, and the Antichrist, the final invader will arrive—the King of Heaven Himself. This will be the most dramatic event in world history.

reflection/discussion questions

1. Describe the Antichrist's character and conduct. How will he gain power? How will he control Israel?

2. Describe the prevailing conditions during the first three-and-a-half years.

3. List some of the catastrophes that will occur during the second half of the Tribulation.

4. Who are the 144,000 and the two witnesses?

5. Who are the armies at the Battle of Armageddon?

Chapter 19

THE RETURN OF JESUS CHRIST

The term, "Second Coming," evokes images of power and grandeur. We envision Christ slaying the Antichrist by the word of His mouth and stopping the greatest battle of all time. The book of Hebrews says Christ shall "appear again unto salvation" (Hebrews 9:28), but this salvation is not in reference to sin. Jesus' Second Coming is not for the purpose of delivering man from condemnation. He accomplished that at His first coming. This time, He will deliver the world from the presence of evil.

Jesus had told His disciples what to expect (Matthew 24:23-26). They were emblematic of the nation of Israel during the Tribulation period. The apostles, of course, did not go through the Tribulation, but they represent Israel. Jesus told them, "If anyone says to you, 'Behold, here is the Christ,' or 'There He is,' do not believe him, because false Christs and false prophets will arise and show great signs and wonders so as to mislead if possible even the elect. Behold, I have told you in advance. If therefore they say to you, 'He's in the wilderness,' don't go forth, or 'Behold, he's in the inner rooms,' don't believe them." In that day, people will say the Messiah has come, but they are liars. When He returns, no one will have to tell anyone!"

Jesus then described in verse 27 how He would appear: "Just as lightning comes from the east and flashes to the west, so shall the coming of the Son of Man be." His coming will not be secret, it will not be private, and it will not be something people have to take by faith. It will be like bolts of lightning shooting across the sky!

Luke records one of the apostles asking Jesus, "Where Lord?" Jesus answered, "Where the corpse is, there will the vultures gather" (Luke 17:37). This is a reference to Jerusalem which will be like a dead body surrounded by predators. Christ's coming will spare Israel from imminent, certain, and inescapable doom and despair.

Matthew 24:29 describes the conditions that surround the appearing of the Son of Man: "Immediately after the tribulation of those days, the sun will be darkened, the moon will not give its light, the stars will fall from the sky, and the powers of the heavens will be shaken." Why will all these heavenly lights disappear? Jesus explained, "Then the sign of the Son of Man will appear in the sky." During the day, you cannot see the stars because the greater light of the sun dims them. That possibly is the meaning of this verse. Revelation says, "The skies will be rolled back like a scroll." Isaiah calls to God, "Rend the heavens and come down." That's what happens at the Second Coming (Isaiah 64:1).

I don't think people will immediately see Jesus Christ. First they will see the angelic hosts, then they will see the appearing of "the spirits of just men made perfect"—the Old Testament saints (Hebrews 11:23). Next they will see the armies of heaven in fine linen, bright and clean—the glorified church (Revelation 19:14). Finally, they will see the brilliance of God's glory that is called in the Old Testament the *Shekinah*. John, Ezekiel, Daniel, and Isaiah all fell over "like dead men" in its presence. Solomon and his priests fled the temple when God showed Himself. It is a glory no man can look upon and live.

Jesus continued His explanation in Matthew 24:30, "All of the tribes of the earth will mourn, and they will see the Son of Man coming on the clouds of the sky with great power and glory." It is a sad thing to be in the presence of the One who reveals their ignorance and folly, and to have no hope.

Round TRip

In the book of Acts, as Jesus ascended into heaven from the Mount of Olives, an angel appeared and asked the disciples, "Why, oh men of Israel, are you gazing into the sky? This same Jesus whom you see departing will come in the same way as he left" (Acts 1:11).

Zechariah 14:3-4 states, "Then the Lord will go forth and fight against those nations as when He fights on a day of battle, and in that day His feet will stand on the Mount of Olives." The Mount of Olives is east of Jerusalem. When Christ returns, it will be split from east to west and form a large valley. Zechariah concludes, "You will flee by the valley of my mountains," that is, the valley created when the Mount of Olives is split.

In the Roman Empire, after a battle had been won, the victorious general often rode home on a white horse. Similarly, Jesus Christ will come to the Battle of Armageddon on a white horse (Revelation 19:11). Christ's victory is assured even before the battle begins

Revelation 19:20 states, "And the beast was seized and with him the false prophet who performed the signs in his presence, by which they deceived those who received the mark of the beast and those who worship his image. And these two were thrown alive into the lake of fire which burns with brimstone." In II Thessalonians 2:8, Paul said of the Antichrist, Christ "will slay by the sword of his mouth and bring to an end by the appearance of His coming."

Christ then will send forth His angels to gather the nation of Israel. In the Mosaic Covenant (Deuteronomy 28), God had warned that Israel would be banished from their land if they fell into idolatry. They did sin, they were banished, and they have been excluded from the land. Even today, the Jews are not the sole possessors of their land. Deuteronomy 30 was an assurance to Israel that they would someday be gathered into their land. Deuteronomy 30:1 begins: "It shall be, when all of these things have come upon you, the blessing and the curse which I have set before you, and you called them to mind in the nations where the Lord your God has banished you, and you returned to the Lord your God and obey Him with all your heart and with all your soul according to all that I command you today, you and your sons." The only condition God gives for the nation of Israel to be gathered is for them to repent. Through the Tribulation, Israel will learn to say, "Blessed is He who comes in the name of the Lord."

Verse 3 promises, "Then the Lord your God will restore you from captivity, have compassion on you and gather you again from all the peoples where the Lord your God has scattered you. If you are outcast or at the ends of the earth, from there the Lord your God will gather you, and from there He will bring you back. And the Lord your God will bring you into the land which your fathers possessed, and you shall possess it, and you will prosper, and he will multiply you more than your fathers." This promise is called the Palestinian Covenant.

The Palestinian Covenant's promise that Israel will be gathered has never occurred in the way this text illustrates. Verse 6 describes the regeneration of the nation when the New Covenant will be enacted upon the people of Israel: "Moreover the Lord your God will circumcise your heart and the heart of your descendants to love the Lord your God with all your heart and with all your soul in order that you may live." Also, God will inflict curses upon their enemies if Israel will remain true to Him.

BEHOLD THE BRIDEGROOM!

Once the nation is back in the land, the judgment of Israel begins. In Matthew 25:1, Christ compares Israel to ten virgins. In those days, weddings were somewhat different than those today. They were a picture of our salvation. The father chose the bride and arranged the marriage. Then during a betrothal period, the groom gave the bride a down payment assuring that he would follow through with his commitment to marry her. The father's role was to protect her and present her as a virgin. The bride wore a veil as a symbol of her virginity. The invitations were sent, and the bride made herself beautiful. The groom had prepared an apartment in his father's house. He took his bride to a bridal party, and waited at the bridal party as long as she wanted to stay there. While they were at the party, the groom's friends went to his house and waited for the bridal procession. The groom was placed on a chair and carried. The friends of the bride held up lamps and waited for her. They didn't know when she was coming, but they always had to be ready. When she appeared, the two would go into the bridal chamber and consummate the marriage. Then the couple came out and joined the party. Then they all celebrated at the wedding feast. The beautiful bride was the glory of her father's love because he had given such a beauty to this young man.

Similarly, we are chosen by the Father, and we are redeemed and betrothed by Jesus Christ. He has gone away to prepare a place for us while we are getting ready to join Him. He's given out invitations for everyone to come to a wedding feast. Someday He will come and get us, and the Father will present us to the Son as a spotless virgin.

In Matthew 25, Israel is pictured as virgins, "friends of the bride," waiting for the appearance of Christ and His church. "Then the kingdom of heaven will be comparable to ten virgins who took their lamps and went out to meet the bridegroom." Every Jew knew what that meant. They never knew when the bridegroom was coming, so they had to be ready. "Five of them were foolish and five were prudent, for when the foolish took their lamps, they took no oil." That was dumb! Why would they take lamps without oil? The answer is: they didn't think he would come quickly, so they procrastinated. But he appeared, and those who left to find oil weren't allowed in the wedding feast when they got back. This is a picture of Israel today. When the Tribulation starts, Israel had better be ready because the Bridegroom is coming soon! Those who are not ready are pictured as unbelieving Israel; those who are prepared are the true, believing remnant.

finishing touches

Jesus then describes the judgment of the Gentile nations in Matthew 25:31: "When the Son of Man comes in His glory and His angels with Him, then He will sit on His glorious throne, and all the nations will be gathered before Him." At this time much of the earth has already been destroyed. Not many people are still alive, and Jesus will gather to Himself the remaining nations. He will judge them and separate the sheep (the believing Gentiles) from the goats (the unbelieving Gentiles) who received the mark of the Beast and refused to assist Israel.

Jesus said of the judgment, "These will go away into eternal punishment, but the righteous into eternal life" (Matthew 25:46). This will be one of the most dramatic events of history as unbelievers pass away into eternal punishment. But afterward, a purified Israel and a purified Gentile nation will be ready for the kingdom.

When Christ begins His kingdom, no evil people will exist. There will be no traitors among earth's people. Zechariah 13:2 says of this period of time: "God will remove from the land the unclean spirit," that spirit which animates the world.

In Revelation 20:1-3, an interesting event is depicted: "I saw an angel coming down from heaven having the key of the abyss and a great chain in his hand, and he laid hold of the dragon, the serpent of old." This identifies Satan as the serpent from the Garden of Eden. He is the problem from Genesis 3 all the way through history. He will be placed in a pit for a thousand years. "And He (Christ) threw him into the abyss and sealed it and shut it over him so that he should not deceive the nations anymore."

When will this happen? Is Satan bound now, as some would have you believe? One theologian said, "If he is bound now, he must have a long chain because he is still wreaking havoc with the world!" No, this is a prophetic text. It hasn't occurred yet. After Satan is bound, we will go into the kingdom.

Believers will rule with Christ for a thousand years. Saints who died in the Tribulation will be resurrected, and according to Daniel 12:3, Old Testament believers will rise as well. Faithful Old Testament people looked ahead to the kingdom of the coming Messiah. They waited for the fulfillment of the Abrahamic Promise which would ultimately be fulfilled in that day.

Revelation 20:4 says, "And I saw thrones, and they sat upon them and judgment was given to them." Who are these people who rule with Christ? "And I saw the souls of those who had been beheaded because of the testimony of Jesus and because of the Word of God. And those who had not worshiped the beast or his image and had not received the mark on their forehead and upon their hand, they came to life and reigned for a thousand years. The rest of the dead did not come to life until the thousand were completed."

The kingdom will be ruled by three different groups of people: the church, the martyred Tribulation saints, and Old Testament saints. A small number of survivors, Jew and Gen-tile, enter the kingdom. They will multiply, and the earth will take on a splendor which fulfills Old Testament prophecy.

At the wedding feast, people will look at the beauty of the believers, glory in the worthiness of the Son, and marvel at the greatness of the Father who chose us. Blessed are all those who are invited to the wedding feast!

reflection/discussion questions

1. Imagine seeing the Second Coming with the angelic hosts and glorified believers with Christ. How do you think the armies at the battle and the other people on earth will respond when they see this incredible spectacle? Explain.

2. Imagine returning with Christ to win the battle and set up the kingdom. How do you think you will feel and act?

3. How might your actions now determine your place and role in the kingdom?

Chapter 20

THE
KINGDOM

The Bible contains much prophecy about the kingdom of God. Psalm 2 says of the Messiah, "I will give you a rod of iron. Ask of me, and you will rule the nations with it, and you will crush them as one crushes an earthenware jar." The book of Revelation says of Jesus' return, "The kingdoms of this world have become the kingdoms of our Lord and his Messiah."

Many of us have heard such statements, but aren't quite sure what they mean. Frankly, there is a disparity of opinion even among conservative theologians, which makes many people reluctant to teach on this topic. One view considers the kingdom passages to be allegories. They teach that the events are taking place right now—but in a symbolic way. This view requires taking the Bible literally in some places and figuratively in others. Yet another view teaches that the church will bring in the kingdom as a time-space entity in history.

My belief is that we should take the Bible simply and literally. When it speaks of Christ coming on the foal of a donkey, dying upon a cross, and rising from the dead, we take that as literally true. When Isaiah 53 says the Messiah will be punished for our iniquities, we take that literally. So when the Bible states that Christ will return, institute a kingdom, and rule the world from His throne in Jerusalem, I think we can take that literally also. If I believe His first coming was an actual event, then I must take His Second Coming literally.

I hold to the view that Christ will return with His glorified church prior to His thousand-year reign. I believe this in a very literal sense. This perspective fulfills God's promise to the patriarchs and is a literal, normative interpretation of Scripture.

I think there are four major reasons why we don't hear more teaching that defends a literal interpretation of the kingdom:

1. The Second Coming of Christ and His rule on earth is a supernatural event, and many of us are uncomfortable with the supernatural.
2. Some have been anti-Semitic. The kingdom is the exaltation of the Jews, but they don't want a world kingdom run by Jews.
3. The premillennial view is a very pessimistic view of people and history. It places no hope whatsoever in what man or the church can do. History will be redeemed not by the church but by Jesus Christ and His appearing.
4. Some of us like to spiritualize our faith, but the kingdom is very tangible. Some people don't like the idea that the prophecies of God will become historical and touchable.

God will not let world history end with the destructiveness of Satan. Ultimately man will fulfill the purpose for which God created him in the Garden of Eden. Man does not receive dignity from his power or possessions. His dignity and worth are conferred upon him because he is created in the image of God and has been delegated authority by God. "Thou has made him a little lower than God and doest crown him with glory and majesty and make him to rule over the works of thy hands and put all things under his feet" (Psalm 8). Christ's redemptive work will restore man to his rightful place of honor.

tHe king(dom) is coming

The kingdom will be a truly supernatural event. There are seven incredible aspects of the kingdom:

1. *Satan will be bound for one thousand years.*
When Adam sinned, the kingdoms were handed over to Satan, who is called "the prince of the power of the air" (Ephesians 2:2), "the ruler of this world" (John 14:30), and "the god of this world" who "has blinded the minds of the unbelieving that they might not see the light of the gospel of the glory of Christ" (II Corinthians 4:4). Prior to the inauguration of the kingdom, God must get rid of Satan. Revelation 21:2-3 describes Satan's banishment.

2. *Jesus Christ will be visibly present on this planet.*
Paul promised someday we will see Jesus "face to face" (I Corinthians 13:12). Zechariah 6:9-15 describes earth's final king. The roles of priest and king have never been united in one person because that person would have too much power. The priests came from the tribe of Levi; the kings from the tribe of Judah. As described in the Old Testament passages, a crown was placed on the head of the high priest. They put this crown on Joshua, the priest, as a symbol of who will rule in the kingdom. Verse 12 explains, "Behold a man whose name is Branch. It is he who will build the temple of the Lord, and he will bear the honor to sit and rule on this throne. He

will be a priest on his throne."This is the only time the church and state are to be united. Jesus Christ is both high priest and king who will rule on His throne (Matthew 25:31).

3. *Israel will be exalted.*

In that day the nations will stream to Jerusalem saying, "Let us learn of the law of God that we can walk in his ways" (Isaiah 2:2-4). Jerusalem and its king will be exalted. As much as we long for world peace, it will only occur when the Messiah rules from Jerusalem. Then, in Israel, "The sons of those who afflicted you will come bowing to you, and all those that despised you will bow themselves at the soles of your feet, and they will call you the City of God, Zion, the Holy One of Israel. Whereas you have been forsaken and hated with no one passing through, I will make you an everlasting pride. A joy from generation to generation and you will suck the milk of nations and suck the breast of the kings" (Isaiah 60:14).

Israel will be the joy of the entire world. "Be joyful with Jerusalem and rejoice all you who love her! Be exceedingly glad for her, all who mourn over her, that you may nurse and be satisfied with her comforting breast, that you may suck and be delighted with her bountiful bosom for thus says the Lord, 'Behold, I extend peace to her like a river, and the glory of the nations like an overflowing stream'" (Isaiah 66:10).

Israel is pictured as the mother of all the earth, and in response the earth will bless God because of her. Is this because of the greatness of the Jews? No, it is because of the greatness of one Jew, Jesus Christ, who will return, judge the world, and bring to His nation a bountiful blessing.

4. *The bounty of Israel will be great.*

After captivity in Babylon, the Jews returned to their land. They rebuilt the temple, but it was so small that many people made fun of it. God gave Zerubbabel encouragement through the prophet Haggai that he was involved in something which someday would be glorious. "Thus says the

Lord of hosts, 'Once more in a little while I am going to shake the heavens, the earth, the sea and the dry land. I will shake all the nations'" (Haggai 2:6). All the kingdoms of the earth will bring their wealth to God's kingdom. "They will come with the wealth of the nations, and I will fill this house with glory. The silver is mine; the gold is mine. The latter glory of this house will be greater than the former." Micah states that the Davidic Kingdom will pale in comparison to the reign of the Messiah (Micah 4:8).

The book of Amos says Israel's bounty will be so great in that day that the sower of seed will overtake the reaper. The harvest will be so enormous that by the time the farmer finishes reaping, it is time to sow again!

5. *The world will enjoy peace and plenty.*

Zechariah 14:9 says, "The Lord will be one over all the earth in that day. He shall be one, and His name shall be one." Isaiah 9:6, a familiar Christmas passage, is similar: "A child will be born to us, a son will be given."

Government will rest upon the shoulders of this ruler. "His name will be called wonderful counselor, mighty God, everlasting father, the prince of peace. There will be no end to the increase of His government." Most world governments begin, flourish, become arrogant, sin, and are judged. But this government will have no end because its King will be a benevolent, divine monarch in whom is no corruption.

I like the republican form of government used in the United States because it deters the spread of sin to some extent. In a monarchy, sin can spread very quickly because there are fewer checks and balances. Though the corruptibility of man is inevitable, it moves at a slower pace in a democracy. However, the ideal government is a monarchy whose leader is sovereign and holy. The problem is that no human entity can produce that government. Only the zeal of the Lord of Hosts can accomplish it.

Zephaniah 3:9 states, God "will give to the peoples purified lips that all of them may call on the name of Jehovah, to serve Him shoulder to shoulder." At that time, people will actually be able to "visualize world peace" because it will be real!

In Ephesians 1:10, Paul says the church is "a view to a dispensation suitable to the fullness of the times—the heading up again of all things in Christ." The church is meant to foreshadow the kingdom. If someone wonders what Christ's kingdom will be like, he or she should be able to get a good idea of it by examining the church. People should be able to see a picture of "the dispensation that is suitable to the fullness of times." They should see blacks, whites, Asians, Hispanics, men, women, young, and old—all loving each other. They should see peace in the church as a taste of what they will see in Christ's kingdom.

6. All nations will worship God in Jerusalem.

The Feast of Booths was a commemoration of the Exodus when the nation of Israel used palm branches to build little booths like they used on their journey to the promised land. The ceremony celebrated God's deliverance into His promised land. Zechariah 14:16 says of Jesus' kingdom, "It will come about that any who are left of the nations that went against Jerusalem, will go up from year to year to worship the king, the Lord of Hosts, to celebrate the Feast of Booths." In the kingdom, all nations will send delegates to Jerusalem. The entire united nations will participate in the Feast of Booths, and they will celebrate Israel's King who has brought such bounty to their earth.

7. Nature will be transformed.

Sin has cursed the realm of nature. In an echo of Paul's observations in Romans, one poet said, "Creation groans in a minor key." But God gives us hopeful assurance about a future event. The curse on the natural realm is not permanent, and nature waits for its day of redemption. "It will be set free from its slavery to corruption into the freedom of the glory of the children of God" (Romans 8:21-22). Just as we will be raised from the dead and glorified, so creation will be raised from the dead as well.

A great picture of the eventual redemption of nature is when Jesus Christ the Redeemer rode into Jerusalem on the foal of a donkey. That little colt knew her Redeemer and peacefully led Him in.

Reflection/discussion questions

1. In what ways is man trying to establish his own "kingdom on earth" today through technology, government, and education?

2. Describe the kingdom situation for each of these:

   Christ—
   Jerusalem—
   Israel—
   Satan—
   believers—
   unbelievers—
   those who are born during the Millennium—
   nature—

3. Do you think you will be glad to have the position Christ assigns you during the kingdom? Why or why not?

Chapter 21

one LAST test

During the Millennium, children will be born to the people living on the earth. The population will again increase as the memory of sin, the Tribulation, and Armageddon fades. And yet, one question still remains. Will man finally trust God and renounce Satan?

Years ago, a Bible commentator said, "The Golden Age of the kingdom will last a thousand years, during which righteousness will reign, and peace and prosperity and the knowledge of God will be universally enjoyed. But this will not entail universal conversion, and all professions must be tested." All professions of faith are tested—whether they occur in the Garden of Eden, under Old Testament law, during the church age, or even in the kingdom of Christ. Man will prove once more that evil and enmity with God remain in his heart.

At the end of the kingdom age, we learn that "When the thousand years are completed, Satan will be released from his prison" (Revelation 20:7). The evil one who tempted and deceived Adam and Eve, you and me, and the whole world, will be released to attempt the same thing in that final kingdom. I believe Satan's temptation at the end of the Millennium will be identical to his temptation of Eve the Garden of Eden. His temptation was, "You are not allowed to do everything that you wish. Obedience to God keeps you from being what you could be. Righteousness is harmful to you. Rebellion is the key to really living!"

Satan will be released from his prison and will come out to deceive the nations and gather them together for war. The number of them is like the sand of the seashore. They will surround the camp of the saints in Jerusalem. But fire will fall from heaven and devour them (vv. 8-9).

I believe the people in this passage are the children who are born to the saints who live under the reign of Christ. I do not believe it will be a "magic kingdom" where faith plays no part. Even in this kingdom, people still come to God through faith because they still sin and need to trust in the atonement of Jesus Christ. The Bible says that Christ will "rule that day with a rod of iron" (Psalm 2). The book of Micah says that the Christ "will shepherd the land with a sword" (5:6). Some people will still rebel, but rebellion will always be put down; evil will always be dealt with righteously.

a quick review

In the Garden of Eden, Adam and Eve were created in a perfect estate. God even revealed Himself in human form, but Adam and Eve sinned. Then man was restrained by the law of conscience. Man under conscience refused to repent and was judged by the flood. After the flood, God instituted human government, and at the Tower of Babel, God's will was rejected yet again.

God selected a nation and promised land, blessing, and

descendants to Abraham, Isaac, and Jacob. But Jacob's own sons tried to murder their brother, Joseph. The nation of Israel became enslaved in Egypt. The people were spared from the judgment of the angel of death, delivered through the Red Sea, and entrusted with the blessing of the law at Sinai. But God's promises and His law did not restrain evil.

God led them to the Promised Land and made a prosperous nation of them. They rejected God and worshiped idols, so God judged them for their sin. The northern ten tribes were eventually forced into exile in Syria; the southern two tribes, Judah and Benjamin, were carried to Babylon.

God brought Israel back out of captivity. "At the fullness of the time" (Galatians 4:4), He gave them their Messiah, but they put Him on a cross in the perfect fulfillment of God's will. God then instituted the church age—the period of grace which all the previous ages had pointed to, anticipated, prophesied, and waited for. How have we done in the age of grace? As the hymnist says, man "scorns our Christ, and assails His ways." Mankind hates Jesus, His Word, His cross, His Father, and His people. Even God's grace doesn't restrain man's wickedness.

Some day Jesus Christ Himself will reign on the earth in the glory of His kingdom, but people still won't believe! God has enacted numerous ways to restrain mankind, but we have rejected Him at every turn. He appeared bodily at the Garden of Eden. He let people be guided by their consciences from Cain until Noah. He used threats after the flood. He gave them His holy law at Sinai. He allowed His own Son to be sacrificed at Calvary, and there, He demonstrated the greatness of His forgiveness. When Christ returns and rules for a thousand years, even that won't produce faithfulness in wicked hearts. At least we can be sure of two things: Man is corrupt, and salvation is only by the grace of God. The basis of salvation has always been the same: faith in the shed blood of the Messiah, Jesus Christ. The object, or content, of faith gradually became clearer through the ages until Christ came to earth bodily, but the elect of each age were pronounced righteous because they responded to the mercy of God as promised, in the Messiah who was to come, or in the Messiah who had come.

Forty-two times, the Old Testament states that God "will require man according to his deeds." At this point in history, when God's mercy has been poured out for generations, God finally exercises His supreme judgment. At the end of the Millennium, God will finally separate the good from the wicked in heaven and hell. I'm asked quite often, "If there is a good and just God, why does He allow evil to prevail?" I respond, "God has judged the enemy of the world, Satan, at the cross. He has disarmed him, and Christ has been raised from the dead. The wrath of God has fallen on evil, and we can be forgiven." I also say, "The issue is not, 'Why does God not judge?' but 'Why has He not judged *yet?*'" The Bible teaches that judgment day is coming, but God "is patient with you, not wanting anyone to perish, but everyone to come to repentance" (II Peter 3:9).

tHe fɪnaʟ defeat of satan

Four things will happen at the Great White Throne Judgment, which is God's final judgment of mankind. The first event is found in Revelation 20:10: "The devil who deceived them was thrown into the lake of fire and brimstone, where the beast and the false prophet are also, and they will be tormented day and night forever and forever."

Secondly, the physical universe is dissolved. Verse 11 continues with John saying, "I saw a great white throne." God's throne is white because it is the seat of perfect justice. No one can bribe God. His judgment is true. He is absolutely pure in what He says and what He does. "And [I saw] him who sat upon it, from whose presence earth and heaven fled away, and no place was found for them."

Jesus said, "Heavens and earth shall pass away, but my word shall not pass away" (Matthew 24:35). Peter said that someday, "The elements will melt with intense heat, and the earth and all of its works will be destroyed" (II Peter 3:12). God will not only remove the defiant leader; He will also judge the stage upon which rebellion has been perpetrated—the universe which has been cursed by sin. He will cause every neutron, every proton, every molecule, and every atom held together by the counsel of His will to dissipate.

When this happens, "No place shall be found" for anything in existence (Revelation 20:11). There will be no earth, sun, moon, stars, or planets. All that will be left are God, people's souls, and the eternal books which record the deeds of men and women.

tHe dead sHaLL RISe

The third event of note will be a resurrection. In John 5:38, Jesus said the dead would hear His voice and come forth. This is the time when the wicked will come forth to judgment. All unrepentant people shall be raised and shall have resurrection bodies. There will be no annihilation. The righteous will have a resurrection body to enjoy the splendor of God. The wicked will have a resurrection body to endure His absence.

In John's prophetic vision, he saw the dead, great and small, standing before the throne (Revelation 20:12). They are standing as a prisoner stands before being sentenced. Before God will stand Stalin, Hitler, King Tut, Nimrod, Cain, and all the wicked throughout all of history.

Those who died in complete obscurity do not escape. Even "the sea gave up the dead which were in it" (Revelation 20:13). Those who have died in the ocean, never found or buried, will still come forth.

Revelation 20:13 refers to Hades, the present place of the wicked dead. When nonbelievers die today, their bodies go into the grave, and their spirits pass into a place, according to Luke 16, of "flames, torment, and agony." At the resurrection, their bodies will be raised, their spirits will be reunited with them, and they will stand before the awesome throne of God.

The fourth event is God's judgment. In verse 12, John records that "the books are opened." These books are records of everything people have thought, said, and done. This judgment includes a presentation of evidence as well as the pronouncement of the sentence. Not one word is spoken by the condemned. There's nothing for them to say. There's no argument, no advocate, and no arbitrator. This must be the most eerie event in all of human history. Billions of people will stand together in absolute, dead silence before a Great White Throne, to look at the unchangeable, damning evidence of their lives.

The Book of Life is also opened (v. 15). The Lamb's Book of Life is not a lengthy book like the others. The Book of Life is a volume which contains only the names of people who have placed their faith in Christ. According to Revelation, the Lamb's Book of Life was written before the foundation of the world. There's nothing said about their lives, only the fact that they are found "in Christ."

People have asked, "Why does there have to be an eternal judgment?" In II Thessalonians 1:9, Paul states, "These will pay the penalty of eternal punishment away from the presence of God and the glory of His power." Only an eternal punishment is consistent with the nature of the crime. People were created in the image of God. They have the imprint of the Trinity with conscience and will. They have seen the evidence of God in nature. When they see beauty and order, they must realize that there is an intelligent being that precipitated them. People are surrounded by the wisdom of God. They are provided access to God because Jesus died for them. God has done all a deity can do to save the greatest rebel in the cosmos, man. Yet man has renounced God, even to the point of mocking and scorning the idea of justice.

After the bombing in Oklahoma City, many people quickly determined that swift justice should fall on those responsible for obliterating the lives of children in a day care center and all the others in the federal building. It is difficult to conceive of sufficient punishment for killing 168 unsuspecting people.

Similarly, there is no adequate, finite punishment for what man has done to the Creator of the universe.

eternal torment

Man rejected God's greatest gift; therefore he deserves judgment. "But why," some might ask, "does punishment include eternal torment?"

Hell is a place of torment because man will see the nail-pierced hands of Jesus Christ. The One man renounced is the One who gave His life. How eternally and utterly foolish to reject such love! The apostle Paul said, "If you will confess that Jesus is Lord, you shall be saved." Merely by an act of faith, people could have been saved. Unbelief produces the ultimate shame because people die as rebels, convicted and without hope of appeal. We sometimes quarrel with our mates and spend hours not speaking, but can you imagine an eternity without a hint of love and forgiveness? They can never take away the reproach of being an outcast. They are shamed, dishonored forever. They will be like Lady Macbeth who lost her mind and cried, "Out damned spot!" as she compulsively, but unsuccessfully, tried to remove her reproach.

Man's refusal to believe has renounced the highest joy a human can know, and he can never have another opportunity. The very conscience he used to determine right and wrong (and to reject God's existence) was given to him by God. The very mind which drew conclusions that there are no absolutes was the mind God gave him.

People in hell live in a form of death forever as rebels, ingrates, sinners and fools, and they never can remove the shame. This torment also exists because everything divine has been taken away. There is no planet to enjoy, no air, no family, no food, and no gravity. Wicked men enjoy fraternizing, but there is no fraternity in hell. They didn't receive the Giver, so they don't receive the gifts. And it is unchangeable. They are faced with the maddening reality that it will never ever end.

salvation for the righteous

When kings and queens died in Egypt, their bodies were cleaned in the process to mummify them. As a final act, they put a clay object in the place of the dead person's heart. Across that object they wrote the word "silence." Symbolically, every wicked thing the person had done was sealed in silence. Those deeds would never be brought to the mind of a deity. In the same way, many people hope they can find some way for God not to find out about their wickedness. But He already knows. Only Jesus Christ, by His blood, can cleanse the sins of our past. It's not sinless people who escape the Great White Throne judgment; it is those who turned to Jesus as the one source of forgiveness.

The Bible provides clear insight into what will happen in the final destination of planet earth. I have assurance that I will be in the presence of God—not because of anything I have done, but by God's mercy, I responded to the wonderful news my sins could be forgiven in Jesus Christ. It didn't take a lot of brilliance. All it took was honesty to say that God exists, that I am sinful, and that there is no way I can remove my guilt by myself. I needed a Redeemer.

I know where I will be. How about you?

Reflection/discussion questions

1. Who will be present at the Great White Throne Judgment?

2. How will they be judged?

3. Imagine being an unbeliever there. How would you feel and act?

4. Describe what you think hell will be like for unbelievers.

5. Describe what you think heaven will be like.

Chapter 22

tHe
eteRnaL state

After the Great White Throne judgment, everything evil will be gone. It will be as if the fallen universe, Satan, demons, and evil people never existed. God will then create a new heaven and a new earth, which will be populated by a glorified humanity. Let's examine seven aspects of this eternal state.

1. *The eternal state is marked by "entire sanctification."*
Salvation has many tenses: I *am* saved from the penalty of my sin. I *am being* saved day by day from the power of my sinful nature. And someday I *will be* saved from the very presence of sin.

In eternity, believers have new bodies with no temptation, no sin, no devil, and no death. They are sealed in righteousness, in a state called *impeccability* in which they are not able to sin. I asked one of my professors in seminary if we will have a will in the eternal state. He said we will have a glorified will. I asked him, "Can we sin?" He said we will not be able to sin because we will have both perfect wisdom and a perfect will, or as he said, "the double whammy!"

The concept is similar to asking a person, "Can you put your hand on a red hot burner on a stove?" The answer is "No." Does that mean you're not able to? No, you are able, but you cannot and will not. Your will is sealed in wisdom because you have been through the experience of being burned. In the same way, we will be sealed, unable to sin. Some day we will experience uninterrupted worship and fellowship with God. You and I will experience entire sanctification.

2. We will have a resurrection body.

John said it like this, "It has not appeared what we shall be, but we know that when He appears, we will be like Him." Paul told the doubting Corinthians, "Do you not realize that whatever you sow does not come to life unless it dies?" (I Corinthians 15:36) Like a seed, when we go into the ground, we shall come forth in life. We are "sown in weakness and raised in power." We will be like Christ, and our bodies will be transformed from their vile state "into the conformity with the body of His glory."

Jesus said that in the eternal state we will be "like angels." The body of Christ and the bodies of an angel are able to do some remarkable things. They travel through great distances of space; they pass through mass and matter; Christ could appear and disappear. If those properties are the properties of a resurrection body, it will be an incredible experience indeed! We will live in a perfect state before a God of perfect righteousness. We will not, however, have complete knowledge. We're going to enjoy and learn about God forever and forever.

3. A new creation will exist.

John wrote, "I saw a new heaven and a new earth, for

the first heaven and the first earth had passed away"
(Revelation 21:1-5). This new universe occurs at the end of
the Millennium, after the Great White Throne judgment. The
Tree of Life is there, so plant life will be a part of the new
creation. The River of Life flows down from the very
presence of God, therefore, gravity must exist, too. The
Tree of Life will bear its fruit every month, so there's
some sense of cosmology and cycles in nature, as well as
geography and geology. If plants exist, then perhaps bees and
insects will exist to pollinate them. And animals may live there
as well. We will have complete dominion of the animal realm.
The eternal state will fulfill God's purpose for man, the
purpose which was twisted and distorted because of sin.

4. *We will live in a wonderful place.*
John proclaimed, "I saw the Holy City, the new Jerusalem,
coming down out of heaven from God" (Revelation 21:22).
Jesus said, "I go to prepare a place for you." Paul said, "We are
born of the Jerusalem above. She is our mother" (Galatians
4:26). Hebrews says Abraham was "looking for a city which
has foundations whose architect and builder is God" (Hebrews
11:10).

In his book, The Revelation of Jesus Christ, Dr. John
Walvoord suggests that during the Millennium, this heavenly
city will hover above the earth. During the kingdom,
glorified people will not cohabit down here on earth with
men, but they will live in the city above. At that point, after a
new heaven and a new earth are created, the city will rest on
the new earth.

What will the city be like? It is beautiful: "It comes down
out of heaven from God as a bride adorned for her husband"
(v. 2). When a bride comes down the aisle, everyone stands
and looks at her beauty. This city personifies the people who
live in it. Pre-Israel saints, Old Testament saints who waited
for the mercy of God, New Testament saints, Tribulation saints,
and Millennial saints will all be the bride. We will experience
intimacy with God, and it will be lovely!

The city is also enormous. Verse 16 tells us, "It is laid out as a square, the length is as great as the width, and he measured the city with a rod, 1500 miles. Length, width and height are equal." Some excellent Bible scholars teach that the city will be 1500 miles on each side, but I believe this length describes the perimeter of the city. Each side, then, is 375 miles, the approximate size of Kentucky and West Virginia combined. Even if we use the smaller measurement of 375 instead of 1500 miles on each side, the heavenly city is the largest one ever recorded in the history of man. It even goes up 375 miles high! Many feel the city is like a mountain. On its peak is the very presence of God, and He is the central focus of the city. A River of Life will flow from Him, and a central broadway called "The Street" ascends to Him. This must be an enormous city with an enormous population, because the grace of God has been so wide and searching. In this city are people of every tribe, tongue, and generation of our globe.

The heavenly city is also very safe. It has a wall that is 72 yards high (v. 17). There is no threat whatsoever, and the gates are never closed. God's people shall never fear again.

It is the City of Truth. It has a very high wall with twelve gates (v. 12). The name of each of the Israelite tribes is inscribed on these gates because this is the camp of the saints, the true children of God, the true Israel. There are gates on all four sides, and the wall has twelve foundation stones upon which were written the names of the twelve apostles. The city is founded upon Jesus Christ.

It is a very lovely city. "Its glory was like the glory of God. Her brilliance was as a very costly stone, as a stone of crystal clear jasper" (v. 11). Many other precious jewels are mentioned as well (vv. 18-20). Apparently this city will glow in brilliance throughout the universe (Ephesians 3:10).

One of the greatest wonders in the United States is the Grand Canyon, which is little more than a big ditch! We're amazed at very little things: the beauty of a prism, a rainbow, or a Roman candle. But can you imagine a city, 350 miles in each direction, where God Himself shines in incredible brilliance?

5. *We will enjoy the eternal presence of the saints.*

The saints of God will live together forever. You might ask, "Do you mean we're going to be able to talk to Moses and Elijah?" You bet! Peter did at the transfiguration. Paul tells us we will see our loved ones. I led my daddy to Christ in a hospital room just before he died. I haven't seen him since he became a Christian, but one day I will see my father again. Mothers will see Christian children who died. And if indeed babies are in glory, parents will be able to see the children they never knew.

How old will you be? Moses and Elijah apparently weren't 18 at the transfiguration! That's okay, though. Truthfully, I'd hate to be 18 again! In some way, we'll all be able to recognize each other no matter when people died or how long they lived.

6. *The heavenly city will contain the "beautiful vision of God."*

John wrote, "I saw no temple in it, for the Lord God Almighty and the Lamb are its temple" (v. 22). This is of major significance because the temple has always been a symbol of God's relationship with mankind. There are a total of seven temples recorded in Scripture. The tabernacle in the wilderness was the first place God revealed His presence to men. Later, Solomon built a beautiful temple in Jerusalem, and still later, Zerubbabel rebuilt the temple in the return from the Babylonian captivity. Today, you and I are "temples of the Holy Spirit," and people see God in our lives. During the Tribula-tion, the Antichrist will set himself up as a god by defiling the Jewish temple. The millennial temple will be built by Jesus Christ in His kingdom. But the Eternal City will have no temple made of building materials because God will dwell among His people. He will be the seventh temple. The glory of God illumines the Holy City! Technically, we will not live forever in "heaven" because our everlasting dwelling place will be the Eternal City in a glorified world and universe.

In one of the most marvelous passages in the New Testament, Paul tells the Corinthians that at the end of the kingdom, Jesus Christ "will deliver up the kingdom to the Father, after He has put all his enemies under His feet, the last one being death that God may be all in all." At the ascension of Christ, God the Father gave all authority to Him to rule over all. Someday death will be ultimately defeated. And Jesus, having completely fulfilled His mission, will no longer need to mediate for us. God Himself will then rule His people face to face. At that point, we will be able to look upon Him who "dwelleth in unapproachable light which no man has seen or can see."

What will God look like? Paul said he knew a man (referring to himself) who was caught up into the third heaven in the presence of God, and he "saw things of which a man is not permitted to speak" (II Corinthians 12:4). The Bible never tells us what God looks like because we would be like little children trying to comprehend mature questions of life. A small child cannot understand the beauties of being married, for instance. So God reveals Himself to human minds, but we can't fully understand the unfathomable beauties of heaven until we get there. Then we will experience what the psalmist described: "In Thy presence is fullness of joy; in Thy right hand are pleasures forever" (Psalms 16:11).

7. We're going to eat.

Aren't you glad to know that? John records, "He showed me a river of the water of life, clear as crystal coming down from the throne of God and of the lamb, and in the middle of the street, and on either side of the river was the tree of life bearing twelve kinds of fruit yielding its fruit every month, and the leaves are for the health of the nations" (Revelation 22:1-2). There will be no Tree of the Knowledge of Good and Evil, because there will be no need of a test. Yet people will enjoy the tree of life which is a symbol of the provision of God. The Bible has been called bread, honey, water, and milk. We "eat" of it in fellowship with God, and we "eat" of Christ as we enjoy fellowship with Him (John 6:56). In the Old Testament, the feasts of Israel were given to show their relationship with God. In the Eternal City, we will have a feast forever in the presence of God.

When you have a group of people over, where do they migrate to? The kitchen, of course. That's where the sweetest fellowship is! Imagine the gathering of the saints of the ages, with bodies conditioned so there is no need for sleep, during the most marvelous time ever known. We can just enjoy the presence of God—and this goes on forever! I get excited about going to Cancun for three days, so I can hardly think about being in the presence of God forever!

In a very real sense, most of the Bible is between the two "bookends" of Genesis 2 and Revelation 22. Everything in between is a parenthesis of God's blessing in Genesis 2 and restoration in Revelation 22. Revelation 22:3-5 is a mirror image of Genesis 3. In Genesis there was alienation; in Revelation there is fellowship. In Genesis we were under the dominion of sin; here God rules an eternal kingdom. In Genesis people were separated from God; here they see Him face to face. In Genesis we were owned by the devil; in Revelation, God's name is on our foreheads. In Genesis there was darkness; and in Revelation 22, there is nothing but light. Death reigns in Genesis; in Revelation we will have life "forever and ever." That is the last word of history in the Bible.

perceptions of eternity

Which would you prefer: the Garden of Eden or the Eternal City? I prefer the Eternal City. The Garden of Eden included only two people; the Eternal City will contain multitudes. In the Garden, God appeared in bodily form; in the Eternal City, He shines in incredible brilliance. In the Garden, Adam and Eve had a limited knowledge of God; in the Eternal City, we will have a limitless knowledge of God. The Garden was infested with a tempter; eternity will be characterized by righteousness.

Satan thought he had achieved a major victory in the Garden of Eden. But even as God allowed man to fall, He had a plan to raise him up again in the redemption of Jesus Christ. And we are raised not back to a Garden, but to the eternal state. Even man's sin perfectly fits with the sovereignty of God. The Westminster Catechism states: "For His own glory, He hath ordained whatsoever comes to pass." In our final estate, we will glorify God for His every attribute: His goodness, His love, His wrath, His holiness, His purity, His veracity, His unchangeableness, His righteousness, and His justice. We shall see Him face to face, and we shall understand Him far more than ever before.

How will we feel in heaven? I got a clue some time ago after a tragic, freak storm in the Dallas area. I watched a television interview with a man who was an eyewitness when hailstones started falling. He said some were the size of softballs, and they were falling like cannonballs! He also described how several women got caught out in the open. There was no place to go. So to protect them, their husbands turned their wives' faces to them, then the men put their arms around the women to shield them. These men stood between their wives and the storm! The wives could literally feel their husbands shudder when the enormous hailstones hit them. At times, they could hear the cracking of a hailstone against a skull or shoulder blade. Some women felt the blood of their husbands' battered faces run down onto them, but the men stood firm and protected them. Finally, some of the men lost consciousness and collapsed, making sure they fell forward so their bodies would drape over their wives and continue to protect them.

I wondered at the time how these women felt about their husbands when they saw how they suffered. Many of the men will be scarred and disfigured for the rest of their lives. They will have permanent wounds because they held their brides close and protected them. Because of the wounds on these men, surely their wives' love for them will grow and deepen.

I've wondered what we will feel when we stand and look upon the glory, the majesty, and the greatness of God. We will see a Man, and that Man will have the only disfigurement in the universe. Jesus Christ said to Thomas, "Put your finger in my hand, and put your hand in my side, and be not unbelieving, but believing." John saw in glory "a Lamb standing, as if slain" (Revelation 5:6), the Lamb of God and the Lion of Judah. Jesus Christ's disfigurement will stand out as more glorious than any perfection of heaven. Mortal wounds on an immortal Man. And we shall know that He bears those wounds because He clutched us to His side as He stood between us and the gale of the wrath of God. He shuddered, He bled, and He died a death which was intended for you and for me.

When we see Jesus in the Eternal City, we will feel a depth of love more majestic and deep than any family has ever experienced. Such is the intensity and depth of the love between a Father and His children, a King and His subjects, a Husband and His bride. That is a love that you and I have never experienced—yet! We can't understand it now, so we take it by faith. Our relationship with God will be a more romantic and intensely deep love than any husband and wife could ever feel. It is the unique love of a Creator for His redeemed. We now only have an inkling of it. But someday we will experience its fullness. And it shall continue forever.

Reflection/discussion questions

1. What are you looking forward to most about living in the new heaven and new earth?

2. Think back over this study of God's grand design. Has anything surprised you? If so, what?

3. Understanding God's sovereign plan comforts and challenges us. How have you been comforted? How have you been challenged to live wholeheartedly for Christ?

4. What decisions have you made during this study? Who can help you fulfill these decisions you have made?

5. What is the next step for you in your walk with Christ?

Appendix

USING THIS BOOK
in small GROUPS and
sunday school classes

This book is designed to be used individually as well as in small groups. The questions at the end of each chapter provide the basis for stimulating interaction and application of biblical principles.

Many groups are ongoing, and group leaders look for good content to "plug in." These groups can choose to take a chapter of this book a week, or they can cover two or more chapters each week and focus on selected questions from each chapter.

You may want to begin a new group to interact on this material. Consider how you will inform people about the formation of the group. You may want to write a "blurb" for the bulletin or church newsletter, and you may want to make announcements in Sunday school classes. Or perhaps you already know plenty of people you can invite personally. Be sure to explain the benefits the study will provide for them. They need to know their time commitment will be worth it! Also, people in a new group probably won't commit themselves to a 23-week study, so limit the time to 6 to 10 weeks. If they want more time after the 6-week group to discuss the content and the applications, the group can then begin again with a longer time commitment.

Some churches may choose to use this material for Sunday School classes. In this case, books need to be available for people to purchase, and in some cases, books may be provided free of charge. You may want to teach a chapter or two each week, and be sure to provide plenty of time for questions. Don't let the discussion become too academic. Encourage people to apply the principles to their goals, motivations, and relationships.

Application is the key to any successful Bible study. Share examples of your own struggles and successes in learning to apply biblical truths. Remember, a study of the sovereignty of God and His gracious plan for mankind will serve to comfort and challenge people. Let this be the theme of your group or class.

As Paul wrote to Timothy, his son in the faith, "All Scripture is God-breathed and is useful for teaching, rebuking, correcting and training in righteousness, so that the man of God may be thoroughly equipped for every good work" (II Timothy 3:16-17). The goal of a group or class is that God will change lives!

ANCIENT PATHS

> "... ask for the ancient paths where
> the good way lies and there you will
> find rest for your souls."
>
> Jeremiah 6:16

Sometimes I watch this cheapened day . . .
This plastic, shallow, lying way
This dangerous kingdom, far astray
Errant, cocky, scarce at bay

My mind goes back as in retreat
Seeking days 'fore wayward feet
Caused maddened men themselves to eat.
I search for solid ground

Barney, Andy, and Aunt Bea . . .   The Mick and Yogi and Joe D.
Back to Spurgeon, back to right. To Winthrop's God of Pilgrim's sight.
Back to Luther and his way. Fierce, devoted in his day.
To Florence in its day of life. Aquinas' philosophic strife.
Back to Patrick, souls to glean in the land of Kelly green.
The martyr's day of Foxes' Book. Back from where the standard took.
Apologists, the Fathers, all – and
                              Finally, I look to Paul.
Each book, I bathe in perfect light
Defining One, dispelling night
Then I emerge . . . more apt to bear.
                    My standard fixed
                    My hope
                              wrought there.

So come you offbeat errant day
Rot deep and far as eye can see
But I have seen the perfect Way
I've seen what was and what should be.